PRISONS THAT
COULD NOT HOLD

BARBARA DEMING

PRISONS THAT COULD NOT HOLD

INTRODUCTION BY GRACE PALEY
PHOTO ESSAY EDITED BY
JOAN E. BIREN (JEB)

SPINSTERS INK
SAN FRANCISCO

First edition
10-9-8-7-6-5-4-3-2-1

SPINSTERS INK
P. O. Box 410687
San Francisco, CA 94141

Cover Photograph: © Joan E. Biren (JEB)
Cover Design: Pamela Wilson Design Studio
Typesetting: L. A. Hyder and ComText
              Typography, Inc., San Franciso
Production: Robyn Raymer and Debra DeBondt

Publication of this book was made possible through the generosity of Angels Ink.

Printed in the U.S.A.
ISBN: 0-933216-15-7
Library of Congress Catalog Card Number: 85 — 50990

Table of Contents

INTRODUCTION

At the Friend's Meeting House a couple of weeks after Barbara Deming died, we gathered to remember her for one another, to take some comfort and establish her continuity in our bones.

Later our friend Blue gave me two little wool hats assigned to me by Barbara as she worked those last weeks at dying. That work included the distribution of the things of her life, how to be accurate and fair in the giving, how not to omit anyone of that beloved and wide-webbed community. I imagine that when she came to my name, she thought — Grace needs wool hats up there in the north where the body's warmth flies up and through the thinning hair of her head. Besides I noticed that she likes little wool hats — .

"This too," Blue said and gave me an envelope. In it were shards and stones gathered from the rubble of Vietnamese towns in '67 or '68. On the envelope, these shaky letters were written "endless love." Nothing personal there, not "*with* endless love." The words were written waverlingly with a dying hand on paper that covered bits and pieces of our common remembrance and understanding of another people's great suffering. I thought Barbara was saying, — Send those words out, out out into the airy rubbly meaty mortal fact of the world, endless love, the dangerous transforming spirit.

———

This book is the story of two walks undertaken to help change the world without killing it. Barbara Deming was an important member of both. Twenty years of her brave life lie between them. Both walks were about connectedness, though the first began as a Peace Walk — from Quebec to Guantanamo, the American Army Base in Cuba. In Georgia, it became impossible to demonstrate for peace without addressing the right of all citizens, black and white, to walk together down any street in any city of this country. Before the events in Albany, Georgia, had ended — the jailing, the fasts, the beatings — the peace movement and the civil rights movement had come to know themselves deeply related, although there are still people in both movements who do not understand this flesh and blood connection.

The second walk began in the city of Seneca, New York. In 1848 the first Women's Rights Declaration was proclaimed in Seneca. And much earlier, in the 16th century, Native American women had gathered in the area to ask the tribes to cease their warfare. The walk, organized by the Seneca Women's Peace Encampment, continued through upstate towns in order to reach the huge missile base in Romulus. Its purpose was, in fact, to connect the struggles of women against patriarchal oppression at home and at work to the patriarchal oppression which is military power — endless war.

In both cases the walks were bound by non-violent discipline.

Both walks were interrupted by hatred and rage. The walkers in '64 and again in '83 had to decide whether to continue on their lawful way or accede to the demand of the police chief (or sheriff) to take a different, less visible route; to leave the screaming, cursing men and women with their minds set in a national cement of race hatred,

Jew hatred, woman hatred, lesbian hatred, or to insist on the citizens' responsibility to use democratic rights — not just talk about them.

In both cases the decision the walkers made: We will not attack anyone, we will be respectful, we will not destroy anything, we will walk these streets with our non-violent, sometimes historically informative, signs and leaflets. We may be pacifists, but we are not passivists. In both cases a confrontation occurred. It was not sought by the walkers but it was accepted by them.

On that first long journey, men and women walked and went to jail together. Women alone took the second shorter walk and 54 were jailed. Barbara was among them. It was her last action and those who were arrested with her are blessed to have lived beside her stong, informed and loving spirit for those few days. That difference between the two walks measures a development in movement history and also tells the distance Barbara traveled in those twenty years.

The direction her life took was probably established by the fact that her first important love was another women, a hard reality that is not discussed in *Prison Notes* (this is probably the reason she insisted that her letter to Norma Becker be included in any reissue of that book). This truth about herself took personal years in which she wrote stories, poems and became a fine artist who suffered because she was unable to fully use the one unchangeable fact of her life, that she was a woman who loved women.

As a writer myself, I must believe that Barbara's attention to the "other" (who used to be called the stranger) was an organic part of her life as an artist — the writer's natural business is a long stretch toward the unknown life. All Barbara's "others" (the world's "others" too), the neighbor, the cop, the black woman or man, the Vietnamese, led her inexorably to the shadowed lives of women and finally to the unknown humiliated lesbian, herself.

It was hard when this knowledge forced her to separate her life and work from other comrades, most of whom believed themselves eternally connected to her. "Why leave us now?" friends cried out in the pages of "WIN." "Now, just when we have great tasks." She explained — because I realize that just as the black life is invisible to white America, so I see now my life is invisible to you. Of course *she* was not the separator. *They* had been, the friends who wrote, saying "we know it's OK to be a woman" but hated to hear the word "feminist" said again and again. She stubbornly insisted that they recognize Woman and especially Lesbian as an oppressed class from which much of the radical world had separated itself — some for ideological reasons, some with a kind of absent minded "we'll get to that later." (And many did.)

Of course she never separated herself from the struggles against racism and militarism. She integrated them into her thinking. As she lived her life, she made new connections which required new analyses. And with each new understanding, she acted, "clinging to the truth" as she had learned from Gandhi, offering opposition as education and love as a way to patience.

The long letters that Barbara began to write after her terrible accident in '71 have become books. They are studious, relentless, in argument; she seems sometimes in these letters to be lifting one straw at a time from a haystack of misunderstanding to get to a needle of perfect communication stuck somewhere at the bottom. At the same time she had developed a style which enabled her to appear to be listening to her correspondent while writing the letter. In our last conversations, (by phone) she explained that she had decided to discontinue treatment, the agonizing, useless treatment for her ovarian cancer. She had decided she said, to die. "I'm happy now, I'm serene and I want to die in that serenity. I don't want to die in a chaos of numbness and nausea."

She left the hospital and went home to Sugarloaf Key to be with her companion Jane Gapen and the women of that community. To be strongly present when friends came to visit. They came long distances to say goodbye, to stay a couple of days, to be part of the ceremonies of farewell, and passage.

In the end she taught us all something about dying. I thank her for that last lesson and I have written here in the present tense a few other things I learned from her before those last days.

Learning from Barbara Deming:

First: She's a listener.
So you can learn something about paying attention.

Second: She's stubborn.
So you can learn how to stand, look into the other's face
    and not run.

Third: She's just.
So you can learn something about patience.

Fourth: She loves us — women I mean — and speaks to
    the world.
So you can learn how to love women and men.

Grace Paley
August, 1985

PRISON NOTES
1964

ONE

Albany city jail, Georgia. The cop locks the door on us and walks off. Now we're out of mischief. The barred steel door has banged shut; the big key has made a lot of noise; they have "put us away." People still believe there is some magic in the turning of a key.

He walks past some other cages, running his night stick, clattering, along the bars; and then we hear him make a curious little clucking noise to the prisoners—as though human speech were not quite appropriate to cross the distance between us. Magically, now, we are no longer quite of the same species.

As he goes, he glances down at his boots, and he puts his hand—as if to be sure of something—upon his wide leather belt with its creaking tooled-leather holster.

"Sonofabitch cop!" a prisoner rages, and grasps the bars and rattles them. "Oh goddam motherfucking sonofabitch! Wait till I get out of here tomorrow!"

I am reminded of a fairy tale I once heard about a miser and his old slippers. One day they cause him embarrassment and he tries to throw them away. He isn't able to. He throws them out the window, he buries them in the garden, he tries to burn them, he travels to a distant country and drops them in a pond; but each time fate returns them to him, and each time in a way that causes him mischief. They are too much a part of him. If the miser could not get rid of his old slippers . . .

[1

But people persist in believing that they can put other people from them.

Yes, they manage to sound very reasonable to themselves as they talk of deterring others from crime; but the act of putting a man in jail remains essentially the act of trying to wish that man out of existence. From the moment of arrest one begins to feel against one's flesh the operation of this crude attempt at sorcery.

I remember suddenly the first time I was ever arrested, in New York City, 1962. As I begin to write about time I have served in Albany's jail, my earliest impressions of the world of jail crowd upon me.

A bitter March morning. The United States has just announced resumption of nuclear testing, and in protest I have sat down with a group of pacifists in front of the A.E.C. building on Hudson Street. A small group of us sit, expecting arrest; a larger group circles there, immune from arrest, in a simple picket line. The arrests are swift. Before we have time to shiver on the cold sidewalk, we are picked up and dumped into a paddy wagon waiting at the curb. We are dumped into the back, but we crowd that section, and one of the cops tells three or four of us to crawl over into the space up front in the wide cab. Up there we can stare out the open door at our friends walking past, almost within our reach. And they could look in at us easily, exchange a few friendly glances. But not one of them does, though we sit there for quite a long while before we are driven away, and they circle past us, circle past us again. With our arrest, we have become invisible, even to them. My friends are being dignified, of course; but there is more to it than that. When people are arrested, a kind of primitive awe can take hold of everybody involved. They are caught up in spite of themselves in the ritual act of denying our existence.

2]

I remember the woman guard sitting outside the detention cell in which some of us were held before being taken to the Women's House of Detention—remember her uneasiness every time she noted in us signs of life.

She spies dangling from my lapel the lettered white ribbon we have all worn that morning: NO TESTS EAST OR WEST. She snatches for it. "No banners in here!" A little later she says that she can make one telephone call for each of us. One young woman in the group writes out a message to her sweetheart. She makes it, carefully, very brief, but her feeling for him is clear in it—it flies this banner. The guard gives a little start as she reads it, takes a pencil, swiftly edits. Nothing of the young woman's self now remains in the message.

Nobody has to print in a manual for guards that the prisoner must be wished out of existence for society's sake; this magic principle is grasped as if by instinct. Prison routine varies from place to place, but the one blind effort shapes it everywhere. Here is part of the routine of our "admission" that day:

A policewoman takes us into a small room in the building where we are arraigned. She searches our handbags for sharp objects; we take off most of our clothing for her, unfasten the rest as she peers at us. The guard outside the temporary detention cell examines our bags for a second time, removes a few more possessions. At the House of Detention, a third guard empties the bags, keeps every remaining article. We have packed a few things with which to keep ourselves decent: comb, toothbrush, deodorant, a change of underclothes. She takes them all—even, in my case, some pieces of Kleenex. And if I have to blow my nose? "Find something else to blow it on," she tells me cheerfully. She explains then: I might be smuggling in dope this way. I am led into a large shower room and told to strip. Another guard shakes out

[3

each piece of clothing. Hands on her hips, she watches me closely as I take my shower, and I struggle hard now for self-possession. Her stance reminds me a little of that of an animal trainer. Now she asks me to hold my arms wide for a moment, turn my back and squat. I ask the reason. She, too, is searching for dope—or for concealed weapons. One of my companions has been led in by another woman and has stripped and is sitting on the toilet there. Her face is anguished. She explains her predicament to the guard: she is menstruating, but her extra sanitary napkins have been taken from her. "Just don't think about it," the woman tells her. I don't know how to help her; catch her eye and look away. I am given a very short hospital gown and led now into a small medical-examination room. Another of my companions is just leaving the room and smiles at me wanly. I climb up on the table. I assume that the examination performed is to check for venereal disease. The woman in the white smock grins at me and then at her assistant, who grins back. No, this too is a search for concealed dope or dangerous weapons.

I hear myself laugh weakly. Can they frisk us any further now? As a matter of fact, if their search is really for dope, they have neglected to look in my ears, or up my nose, or between my toes. They wouldn't be able to admit it to themselves, but their search, of course, is for something else, and is efficient: their search is for our pride. And I think with a sinking heart: again and again, it must be, they find it and take it.

Sometimes, all of a sudden, one of them will give it back. People are everywhere, happily, unpredictable. I am told to dress again before going to my cell, but I'm not allowed to wear my tights (because I might hang myself with them?) or my fleece-lined English snowboots (these are labeled "masculine attire," forbidden). A

4]

young Negro guard tells me to find some shoes for myself in an open locker she points out. I stare at the heap of old shoes and tell her wearily, "It's hopeless. Most of these have heels and I can't wear heels. Also, my feet are very big."

She looks at me and smiles. She says, "If you thought anything was hopeless, you wouldn't have been sitting down on that sidewalk this morning!"

I smile at her, astonished, and feel my spirits return. I tell her, "Thank you. You're right. I'll find a pair."

Before I can, she kneels, herself, and fishes out some floppy slippers that will do.

But more often the guards are caught up altogether in the crude rite of exorcism. I remember the ride to jail in Macon, Georgia, this past November. We are peace and freedom walkers this time. A number of us who will go to jail again in Albany have been arrested for the crime of handing out leaflets.

The guard who drives the paddy wagon begins to chatter like an excited boy to the second guard as soon as we are locked in, seated in back on the lengthwise metal benches against the sides of the cab. He suddenly lurches the car forward, then, with a gnashing of gears, backward, then forward again, swerving the wheel. Knocked against the metal walls, we link arms quickly; brace our feet, not to be tumbled to the floor. Later we'll meet prisoners who are black and blue from such falls. "Something seems to be the matter with the gear shift!" he shouts, delighting in the pretense. There are railroad tracks to be crossed; he manages some good jolts here by zigzagging, then takes the car on two wheels round a curve. "Yes, something seems to be the matter with this car!" As the drive ends, and he jerks us again in the prison yard, forward, backward, forward, backward, forward, we put out our hands instinctively to touch one another:

[5

you are still there. But the exulting excitement in the driver's voice betrays his opposite conviction: we cannot be people any more. He has shaken that out of us.

Now it is Albany, Georgia. This is the city where the police chief, Laurie Pritchett, likes to boast that he has defeated Martin Luther King nonviolently. When we are arrested for walking peacefully down the sidewalk with our signs, and in protest we sit down, conspicuous respect is shown for our persons: we are carried to the paddy wagon on stretchers. But the familiar instinct persists, for all this show. Ralph has been dumped into the wagon gently enough, and I have, and Kit and Tony and Michele. They are bringing John-i-thin. One cop looks at another. Suddenly they tip the stretcher up, the wrong way round, standing John-i-thin on his head.

Magic: Shake it out of them—the fact that they are people. Or tip it out of them. Or frisk them of it. And put them away. Has the relation with them been a difficult one? Now they don't exist.

Our cage in Albany is seven by seven by seven. Three bolted steel walls, a steel ceiling, a cement floor. For bunks, four metal shelves slung by chains—two on one wall, double-decker, two on the wall opposite. Thin filthy mattresses. No sheets, no blankets, but, very recently, muslin mattress covers have been added. The chief expects publicity, perhaps. Against the third wall, a tiny washbasin. Cold water. Next to it, a toilet without a lid.

The mattress of the lower bunk rests against the toilet. The upper bunk is so close above the lower that one can only sit up on the lower bunk with a curved spine. The floor space allows one to pace one short step—if there are not too many inhabitants. We are six at the moment, but we'll be more. Other cells are more crowded. It is not by stretching out that the prisoner here will recover himself.

The fourth wall is made of bars and a thick barred door, centered in it. In the corridor outside, guards and plainclothesmen come and go, day or night. If one is sleeping, a sudden knock at the bars: "Hey!" Or a little tug at the hair of the sleeper's head: "What's this one?" No corner of privacy in which to gather oneself together again.

The dirty windows in the corridor look out upon an alley and a brick wall. (They are very dirty. A prisoner long ago has flung a plate of spaghetti against one of them. Shriveled tatters of it still hang there. On the window next to it a shrunken condom hangs.) A little weak sunlight filters through to us at certain hours, but there is no real day .

And no real night. Our only other lighting is a naked bulb hanging in the corridor out of reach, and this burns round the clock.

Not enough space. No real time.

From the cage behind us, around the corridor, a man calls to his wife in the cage next to us: "Are you still there?" She grunts for answer. He calls to her: "I'm still here!"

Laboriously scratched in the metallic gray with which our walls and ceiling have been painted are name after name. RUFUS WAS HERE—was "still here." THE MELTON BROTERS (sic) WAS HERE. BOB WIMBERLY. JACKIE TURLEY. "SUPER" NORMON. Was here, was still here. HAWK, to remind himself, has uttered his name seven times, has flown from wall to wall to ceiling to wall.

The cops read the names with irritation. It is cheating for the prisoners to assert in this way that they do exist.

[7

"We hardly get it painted fresh when it's covered over again." FREEDOM! LULAMAE. The names appear where they oughtn't, as cries might issue from under the earth. We have scratched our names, too: QUEBEC-WASHINGTON-GUANTANAMO WALK FOR PEACE AND FREEDOM. EDIE, YVONNE, KIT, MICHELE, ERICA, BARBARA. Later, CANDY and MARY will appear.

The man calls to his wife again. She doesn't answer. He calls again. She doesn't answer. He calls again.

"Yeah."

"Do you love me?"

Very low, very tired, "No. You're no good."

I remember suddenly the first prison cell I ever entered—twenty-six years ago. I entered that day out of curiosity an abandoned New England small-town jail, attached to the old courthouse friends and I were turning into a summer theater. The few cells were like low caves, windowless; the walls were whitewashed rock. In one, I noticed on the uneven plaster of the ceiling, scrawled in candle smoke—or cigarette smoke—the declaration I AM A JOLLY GOOD FELLOW. I tried, that day, imagining myself the prisoner—tried and failed. But the words have recurred to me over the years. Today I think of them again.

Hard work, in here, to feel like a jolly good fellow; and so pride almost requires a man to feel he is the very opposite.

From one cell to another an old man calls to a pair of teen-age boys, just arrived. We have heard a detective talking with them; they're in for breaking into a store. "Who are you?" the old man calls. His voice is slurred with drink.

"I know who I am!" one of the youths shouts.

"I'll show you who you ain't," the old man teases.

"You want me to come over there and whip your ass?" one of them asks.

"I bet you're tough," says the old man.

"You're goddam right."

"You think you're bad, don't you?"

"*Bad, bad!*" asserts the boy.

A little later, "What are you in for?" the old man calls. There is a pause.

"*Murder!*" one of them suddenly shouts.

"What are your names?"

One of them starts to answer and the other cuts in: "The Sizemores," he decides. (Later we'll find that name scratched on the wall of their cell—dated months earlier.) "We're the Sizemores. Ed and my brother Dan and my brother Richard. He's not here. Ed is. I mean I am. And Dan. Don't you know the Sizemores? The Sizemores, man—the meanest motherfuckers in town!" He elaborates upon the theme.

The old man is full of words, half incoherent. Somebody yells at him, "Shut up, Pop, shut up!"

The two boys take it up: "Shut up, Pop!" He begins to beat against the bars.

"Only baboons beat on the bars," one of them yells. "And queers. He's a queer, ain't he?"

And now they launch into an endless obscene tirade against him. Pop returns the compliments. The voices rise in hysterical crescendo. "Talk to my ass awhile; my head hurts."

Both sides tire; there is a lull. I hear the two boys tossing on their mattresses. One of them groans to himself, "Oh God, oh God."

Then it begins again. "I'm the motherfucking superior of you!" the old man suddenly insists. "I'm here because I want to be!" He begins to beat again upon the bars.

They taunt him: "Keep a-beatin', keep a-beatin', beat on, beat on!" The voices swell again, in flood.

Silence. They have tired again. I doze a little; wake. They are calling again. My companions are awake, too, and we stare at one another. The voices are quieter now and contain a different note.

The old man is asking, "Did you mean those names you called me?"

"I did at the time," one of the boys replies.

"How about now?"

A pause. "Give me some reason not to and I'll withdraw them."

Pop relapses. "You're a no-good sonofabitch."

Silence.

And then we hear the young man call out again in a voice suddenly as frail as a child's: "You want to be friends? Heh—you want to be friends?"

"I'd rather be friends than enemies," the old man mumbles—then abruptly declares, "I'm friends with everybody."

Another night: We hear the familiar scuffling, cursing, the slam of the metal door. A drunken officer from the nearby air base has been brought in. "Don't put me in here with that goddam drunk!" he commands. "Get me out of here! Cop, come here! Open this door! Open this door!" A fellow prisoner makes a comment. The officer yells, "Shut that goddam sonofabitch up or he's dead!" His voice shifts to a growl: "I'm going to kick the everloving shit out of you." He screams, "Open the door!" Then suddenly, "Leave it locked, you sonofabitches! Shut up, you're dead." He begins to sob. Then again: "Anybody who moves is dead!" His voice mounts in hysteria.

Somebody calls, "I know you're tough-assed, but take it easy."

10]

The officer breaks into quavering song, to the tune of "Bye Bye Blackbird":

"You can kiss my ass, ya ya!
You can kiss my ass, la la!"

Somebody calls to him, "How long have you been in service?"

"Thirteen everloving goddam years."

"What are you in—I mean, besides jail? The goddam air force?"

"The Peace Corps," he growls. "Shut up, you're dead!" He resumes, "Open the door, open the door!" Then very very quietly, "Open the door!" Then in a yell.

And then suddenly, almost eerily—we stare at one another again—there issues out of the midst of all this clamor that other voice we have heard, frail, childlike: "Heh friend, heh friend," the officer calls. "You think they'll let us out of here tomorrow?"

It is another night—scuffling of feet again, the clanging to of the steel door. Curses. Groans. More curses. A fellow prisoner calls out, "You're a bad-ass, aren't you?" "Yes, I'm a bad-ass," the new man confirms loudly. The familiar exchange of obscenities begins. The voices mount in the familiar rhythm. But in the very midst of it—we have learned now to expect it—the voice alters; he calls: "Say—we're friends now, okay?"

We hear the heavy steel doors of the cages clang open, we hear them clang to, as the cops lock the prisoners in or let them out. These arrivals and departures mark the time for us now—a time which stretches, contracts, no longer tidily divided as it was outside jail. I am always surprised, when I glance at my watch, to learn the hour it is. The rhythm of night, day has been broken, as the

[11

light burns round the clock; and round the clock, too, the cops come and go, the prisoners yell at them and at one another; so that we sleep, when we do, simply in those stretches, whatever the clock says, when the yelling subsides enough to allow it. Mealtimes no longer subdivide a day; we have broken this rhythm ourselves, for my companions are fasting and I take only a part of one of the two meals the jail provides—a meal that is brought not at the beginning or the middle or the end of the day but at four in the afternoon. We count the separate days as they pass, but as we have not yet been tried and sentenced, we cannot yet count: one day less to serve. Time has its own peculiar quality in here, and, marked as it is by these clamorous arrivals and departures, it takes on a quality more peculiar still as we begin to hear prisoners who have been released being brought back into the cells again. Time, it seems, runs nowhere. We are in Hell.

I remember my first experience of this, in Birmingham's city jail, May 1963. This was my first imprisonment of any duration—six days; I had been in jail in New York less than twenty-four hours. My crime in Birmingham was walking half a block, a sign around my neck: "All Men Are Brothers." I had taken part in one of the Negro demonstrations. (The sentence was six months, but the case was appealed, and after six days we were all bailed out.) I was separated, of course, from my companions and put on the top floor of the jail; Negro prisoners were held on a floor below.

A large airy room, in this case. Still a cage in fact, but room to pace. (My friends below have less room—very much less of everything.) And we are even let out of the room at certain times—herded downstairs at mealtimes (three times a day here), very occasionally called down to the visiting room. The matron comes to the door and yells for one of us or all. And sometimes she yells a very particular phrase, calls the name of the prisoner and then adds, "All the way!" This means that the prisoner is being released. Festive phrase! The prisoner hurries to gather up her few belongings; she straightens out her skirt, pats quickly at her hair, grinning, shouts a quick goodbye. I remember Ruth saying goodbye, I remember Flo. I remember . . . It is the middle of the next night. There is a sudden racket on the stairs, the heavy door is swung open, and I sit up on my top bunk to see who will come in. I have been asleep, and for the first moment I feel that I am having a senseless dream. She is wearing a different dress now, but that is Ruth who stands there. Her dress is soiled, she is barefoot, one of her eyes is swollen and she is cursing, her face contorted. "You know what that bitch of a matron did? She slapped me! She slapped me!"

It is two nights later. Racket on the stairs again. The door swings open, and Flo staggers in again. She gives me a funny little sideways smile as she passes—sly and despairing. She wanders distracted for a few minutes in the long aisle between the double-decker bunks, then sinks down on the bunk below me. I fall asleep again, then wake to the sound of splashing water. Flo is squatting in the aisle, her skirts lifted. She suddenly passes out and falls forward, sprawled in the puddle she has made. A section of thick glass is set into the floor at that spot, and the feeble greenish light that glows through it from below outlines her there, helpless, her red curls unraveled, her dress twisted, her frilled petticoat showing.

Now in the Albany city jail we hear derisive shouts, welcoming back a man who has been released three days before. He begins at once to curse at someone: "If your brains were made of cotton, there wouldn't be enough to make Kotex for a red-eyed beetle!"

[13

The cop who has brought him in, on his way out, strolls back past our cell, hitching his pants. The look on his face asserts: A job well done; our city is safer now. He slaps his hand against his pistol holster, as if to reassure himself: Yes, there is power in me; I am a member of the force.

No wonder you touch yourself for reassurance.

I think of the heavy doors shutting, the heavy doors opening. First the rite of casting them out of existence. It is time they serve, not eternity, so then the rite of returning them to society. "All the way! All the way!" A cry in a dream. Punishment can almost convince a man that he doesn't exist; it cannot make him feel, Now I am one of you. If society was embarrassed by them before, will it be less embarrassed by them now?

TWO

WE ARE not let out of our cage, day or night. There is no mess hall in this jail; my one meal is shoved to me in a tin plate along the floor under the door's lowest bar. (Usually bologna, which I leave; grits; black-eyed peas; a slightly bitter diced vegetable which I suppose is turnips.) Our toilet is there in the cell. (If a guard comes by while one of us is sitting on it, we hold up a coat for a screen.) There is no prison yard. We get our only exercise climbing up and down from the top bunks. (And Erica, with determination, once a day, stands in the narrow space between the bunks and brings up her knees to her chin a few times.) Here we are. We sit on our bunks or we lie on our bunks.

We sit and listen to the life about us in the jail. We can see from our cage only the corridor outside and, through the row of dirty windows, the alley, the brick wall. But to our ears the prison, all on one floor, lies open—except for one distant room, "the hole." Acoustics play strange tricks, and it's hard to locate exactly from where it is the voices come, but we can shout back and forth to the men in our group—even to Ray and Ronnie and Tyrone, in a segregated cell because they are Negroes. We don't shout very often, because it takes a lot of energy. But Ray, several times a day, sings out to us: "Oh-oh freedom! Oh-oh freedom!" Sometimes we join in, sometimes we just let his single voice roll down the corridors, around the various corners, into all the cells.

[15

Now and then the other prisoners call to us. Most often they call to Yvonne. Something in her voice intrigues them.

"Eevon!"

"What?"

"Do you have any cigarettes?"

"No—I'm sorry."

"All right."

When Candy arrives, they call as often to her—intrigued by her name, of course, and by her youth: she is only seventeen.

"Candy, you there? You all right, baby?"

"Yes, I'm fine. Thank you."

"All right."

But mostly they call back and forth to one another—teasing, cursing, or appealing. Or they talk or groan to themselves.

We talk among ourselves, too, but for long stretches we sit in silence, listening. I look at my friends and see their faces marked by a kind of awe. I recognize it. I remember suddenly the night I left jail after my first brief imprisonment in New York—bailed out, to my surprise, in the middle of the night. I remember walking away, up Greenwich Avenue, turning and turning to look back at the high gloomy building there, my feet, in spite of me, dragging, drawn to retrace my steps and at least touch the walls of the prison; turning to touch it with my eyes, and wondering as I lingered at the strength of my feeling that I was walking away from something of which I was deeply a part.

We sit and listen to the cries, the groans, the curses. Who has not at some time uttered that groan, uttered essentially that curse, of one estranged from others and from his own groped-for life? Those who have thrown us in here wanted to dispose of us; but instead of throwing us out of society, as they would have liked, they have admitted us, by their act, into its inmost room. Here are men and women at their weakest; here, too, society confesses itself at a loss. These are people with whom it has been unable to cope, whom it has been unable to sustain.

A cop unlocks the heavy door of our cell and pushes in with us a pretty curly-haired young woman who has been arrested for drunkenness. She presses her body against the bars as he retreats, shrieking after him. She pulls off one of her pretty white cowgirl boots and begins to bang at the bars with it in a tantrum. The paper drinking cups we have lined up there spill to the floor and roll. Our underclothes, which we have washed and hung there to dry, are scattered too. A button goes flying off her boot into the corridor.

We try to calm her, ask her questions about herself. She quiets down for a moment but then begins to rage again: "I'll kill them all, kill them all!" She takes a bobby pin from her hair and, reaching around the door, begins frantically to try to pick its lock. We point out that it's hopeless, laugh at her gently, and she finally begins to laugh too, her tantrum dissolving—though she picks away for a little while still.

Leaning against one of the bunks, then, she tells us about herself: "I was married at fourteen. . . . Seven miserable years with him. . . . I'm nothing but a whore, I suppose. . . . I called my mother the other day; she sounded just like my enemy." Turning her eyes on us, lost, shining: "I never had any kind of life."

In the cell next to us for a while is a young traveling salesman, member of a fly-by-night company that has been doing something illegal in town. After he has told us with good humor that if our peace walk came through his town and "started a ruckus" he'd just as soon shoot us "as anyone" ("A kid I won't shoot, but if it's a grown-

[17

up I don't care if it's a man or a woman"), he goes on to describe his manner of life to us a little, to tell us of the good times he and the others in his company have, as they move in a group from one motel to another: "We don't know till we jump where we go. . . . We have a ball"—lying in bed and ordering chicken dinners and watching television, each with a girl on call. "The boss keeps our money for us. Saturday night he doles it out. We shower up and go to the honkytonk. Everybody gets drunk." The recitation of his joys is almost as sad as the young woman's recitation of her sorrows; he is so hectically eager to have us believe in them.

One night two cops unlock our door and steer into the cell a drunken weeping woman, huge as a sow, with pendulous belly, pendulous chins. Tears run from the corners of her eyes and black rivulets of snuff from the corners of her mouth. She stands blindly in the small space between the bunks, staring at us, confused; then sinks, like a mountain sinking into the sea, onto a lower bunk we have quickly cleared. We take off her shoes for her. She suddenly reaches out her hand toward me and I take it and she begins to tell us about herself: "I am so old. . . . My husband . . . doesn't love me . . . My grandchildren . . . ashamed of me. . . . I'd like to be pretty like all of you. . . . I am so old." We ask her how old she is. Fifty. We tell her that isn't old. One of us asks why she doesn't see a doctor if it bothers her to be fat. She has been to see a doctor. "He laughed at me." Have we anything to eat? Have we any snuff?

In the distance a Negro woman begins to cry: "Oh, my baby! Let me go home to my baby! Oh, help!"

The fat woman grips my hand more tightly. What are we in for? We tell her about our Walk. "You didn't walk with niggers, did you?" she asks, frightened. "They have more than whites do, you know it—better schools, better

18]

everything. I have a cook, she's a nigger, and she says she wouldn't want things different." Her eyes implore us. Suddenly she falls asleep.

She wakes, turning in bed, groaning "Have you really walked all this way?" And then, in a voice that is almost a whisper, "Girls, I want to ask you something. Did you ever do anything you were so ashamed of you didn't know what to do?"

Yvonne tells her, "No, I believe you do things because you can't help it."

She whispers to us, "Do you think it's very wrong to go with a young boy? My husband doesn't love me. One day I just couldn't stand it any more. . . . The boy was only twenty-one. I got him to drive into the country. We went into the back room of a church." She ends, her voice flat: "He couldn't do anything." The tears begin to run from her eyes again.

We stare at one another, helpless; and I stare again at all the names scratched on these walls: BOBBY. LINDA. JIMMY. DAVID. RUFUS. Over the toilet someone has scratched an arrow and THIS WAY OUT. High up in the corner of the wall next which the woman lies, in letters slanting down, someone has scratched: FOR GOD SO LOVED THE WORLD . . .

I remember suddenly a woman in the Macon jail— Evelyn, in and out constantly for drinking. A handsome, restless woman, she moves to and fro about the room (in Macon's jail there is space in which to move), conversing with herself when not with us, to keep up her spirits, making a kind of bitter fun of herself and of her plight. A plane passes close overhead, and we all stop what we are doing to listen to it. Evelyn raises her arms—marked with dark bruises where the cops have been rough with her— and cries out: "Mr. Pilot! Mr. Pilot! Here I am! Help me! Take me away!" The plane passes on, high overhead,

[19

the humming of its motor growing fainter. "Mr. Pilot!" she cries. "Oh, come back, come back, don't leave me! Come back and get me, Mr. Pilot!" She throws herself upon her cot—"Mr. Pilot, Mr. Pilot!"—half laughing, half weeping loudly. "Oh, why are you abandoning me?" We laugh too, we almost weep too. Her comic cry is the cry of almost all in here, a cry everybody knows, the cry in uttering which Jesus took on the flesh of every person born: "My God, my God, why hast thou forsaken me?"

I remember again the first hours I ever spent in jail— in the New York Women's House of Detention. We have been questioned, fingerprinted, photographed, and searched one two three four five times. The elevator doors open and we step out into the ward to which we have been assigned. The doors open and the scene explodes upon us, explodes within us. The clamor of bedlam bursts in our ears—wild giggles, shrieks of rage, distracted pratings. The motions of bedlam meet our eyes. It is the hour just after dinner; the women have not yet been locked in twos in their cramped cells for the night. They wander in the halls like lost spirits, some of them dejected, heads hanging, others running here and there, others clinging together, amorous—timid about this, some of them, some of them eager to be noticed. They roll their eyes in our direction to see who we are. "Where did they pick *them* up? Look, look." And there also bursts upon us the strong smell of the place—disinfectant, bad cooking, sweat, urine, and something more than this: that special distillation of the flesh of those who are miserable, the smell, simply, of human desperation.

We have missed the dinner hour but are given a hasty meal by ourselves in the mess hall, while a prisoner sloshes a mop about the place. On each tin plate a very sticky mass of macaroni and a large turd which we decide is a fishball. The stuff is hard to swallow; we dump most of it into the garbage pail which stands in the hall.

Then it is time for all to be locked in their cells. I am given a cell with one of my fellow pacifists. Two cots, side by side, a toilet (an empty bottle floats in it), a tiny basin with cold water and no stopper. During the day the one cot can be pushed under the other; when they are side by side, no floor space remains. We talk a little, then try to settle down. This jail provides sheets, but they are the size of crib sheets and don't stretch the length of the mattresses. I feel in spite of myself that I share the bed with prisoner after prisoner who has slept here before me, sweated on this mattress, wept on it, exhaled her despair, been sick, been incontinent. I have undressed and put on the knee-length prison nightgown that has been given to me, but I decide now to put my underclothes and my skirt back on. And I try to curl up so that no part of me touches the mattress itself. And as my flesh shrinks from the touch of certain things here, my spirit shrinks from contact with the life about me. The prisoners are calling to one another from their row of cells. Much of the language is unfamiliar slang, but the cries sound to me lewd and abandoned. I think with despair: See to what a hardly human condition the human being can be reduced. In a delirium of depression, I begin to laugh. My companion has turned her face to the wall. A guard yells at the women to stop their racket—there is supposed to be no talking after a certain hour. The place hushes for a moment. Then some giggling begins.

Suddenly there is a shriek: "What's this in my goddam bed? Matron, turn on the light, turn on the light!"

"It's probably Mickey the mouse," someone calls. "Old Mickey never fails."

There is more giggling, and a great deal of commotion in that cell. Then another hush.

Then suddenly from the cell across from me a woman imitates the plaintive, rather delicate miaowing of a cat. A pause. "Moo! Moo!"—sad and low. And from another dark cell, staccato: "Oink! Oink!" "Baa! Baa!" trembles the length of the corridor. And then a rooster's voice bursts the air in prolonged fireworks: "Cockadoodle doodle doodle doodle doodle doo!"

My depression is scattered. I feel all at once light of heart and no longer set apart in spirit from these others, able to feel for them only pity and distaste.

Someone calls, "Good night, Joan," and someone, "Good night, Lola."

"Good night, Doris!"

"Good night, Cookie!"

"Good night, Toots!"

My cellmate is sitting bolt upright, smiling, and I guess from her look that her feelings now are something like mine. She is a young college girl, very bright and very grave, with heavy glasses, a somewhat peaked look. We nod at each other mutely and she lies down again in bed.

I sit there, leaning my head against the wall, listening. From the small window over the toilet, sounds of traffic far below enter our cell—very clear. Down the corridor I hear the small sounds of prisoners turning in bed or stirring, sighing. I sit there a long time, a peculiar joy rising in me, my sense of distance from all the others here more and more dissolving, a sense of kinship with them waking in me more and more. I reach out and grasp one of the bars of the cage with my hand. I have only to remember that gesture . . . I feel a queer stirring in me, and it is as though my heart first bursts the bars that are my ribs, then bursts the bars of this cell, and then travels with great lightness and freedom down the corridor and into each stinking cell, acknowledging: Yes, we are all of us one flesh. This motion of my heart seems, in fact, so very physical that when I hear my companion turn in her bed, I decide abruptly: this disturbance in the air may frighten her. I call it back into its cage and sit trembling.

I hear a little sound from her. Is she weeping? I whisper, "Are you all right?"

She whispers, "Oh yes, oh yes! You?"

I whisper, "Yes."

I lie now in this cage in Albany, Georgia. There are eight of us, and four bunks. Candy and Mary have been arrested too, and are with us. We have asked for two extra mattresses and been given them and they are on the floor. Three people lie there, closely side by side, legs under one bunk, heads half under another. The third person has her coat over her head because she lies right next to the toilet. I lie alone on a lower bunk tonight; it is my turn to stretch out. From the bunk above me, Edie's thin foot dangles in the air, and in the crack between that bunk and the wall, Erica's square hand is visible. I am not always so sure which limb belongs to whom.

We lie and listen to the cries, the groans, the curses. We are all of us wakeful tonight, but heavy-headed too. No window has been opened for a long time, and the air is thick. A cop has just taken a bottle of corn liquor off someone he has brought in and poured the stuff out in the corridor. The fumes of this spread, too. The man who has been brought in is screaming, "Oh get me out of here, get me out of here!"

I remember suddenly the legend of the Harrowing of Hell. After Jesus, dying on the Cross, cried out that he felt abandoned, the rocky foundations of hell are supposed to have been tumbled out of place; and before he ascended into heaven he is said to have gone down into hell to gather all those spirits who wanted to be gathered.

I think: Let the foundations of every jail that exists

be tumbled out of place—let these hells be harrowed, let them be emptied. I think of all the men and women cast, for a time, into this damnation, and marked by it. I think of their troublesome return to society. I think of the senseless attempt to build heaven more securely by creating hell. The one region can never be shut off from the other. I remember Debs' statement: "While there is a criminal element, I am of it; while there is a soul in prison, I am not free"—not a sentimental statement but a simple statement of fact. I think: The only way to build anything resembling heaven, the only way to build "the beloved community," is to seek again and again not how to cast out but how to gather, is to attempt to imitate Jesus' action. I remember Evelyn again, whom we met in Macon's jail. "We need more company," she had said at one point: "I'm going to ride the broom." A battered broom stood leaning against the wall in a corner, and she straddled it and trotted energetically back and forth the length of the room. This was supposed to be a kind of magic to bring more company in. I think: Yes, ride the broom, ride the broom! Ride it until you have ridden all in who are outside! For if any live in hell, then all do. "We are members one of another." Let them all know this place. When they know it, let them cry out. Then let the walls fall!

24]

THREE

THERE is a jail within a jail here, hell within hell. The men and women behind these bars are not supposed to exist, but some are supposed to exist even less than others.

A prisoner who has just been brought in screams in panic. An old-timer calls to him from a cage around the corner: "Take it easy!"

"You goddam black sonofabitch," cries the newcomer, "you kiss my ass!"

Silence. Then, "How you know what color I is?" the Negro asks softly.

"Fuck you, chocolate drop, I know you're black. Don't talk shit to me; I'm white, I'm the aristocrat. My God, you wish you could change white, don't you?" His voice speeds up. "All you goddam niggers wish you were white! You don't show me shit, you black bastard. You ain't even a son of God, you son of the Devil!" He erupts in what is supposed to be an imitation of the other man's speech: "Blah blah blah blah blah blah blah—"

The Negro answers him wearily, "I don't give a damn if you *blue*; you in jail."

"I'm in jail and I'm blue," the white man suddenly states blankly—for a moment confronting the facts. Then he begins to rattle the bars in another fit. He yells, "Let my ass out of here, you bastards!" He screams again. And again he turns his attention to the other prisoner, for relief. "Where's Martin Luther King at tonight? He going to get you out of jail? Where's old Martin Luther at?" He offers a few obscene suggestions as to where King might be. "You goddam gob of spit," he suddenly cries. "You would like to be white, you Martin Luther King! *Least I don't run round wanting to be black and segregating with you sons of bitches. Least I don't run round sitting on my knees praying up to heaven:* 'Turn me white, turn me white!' Nigger!" he screams; and then with all his breath, "Niggggggaaaaaaaaa!"

My companions jerk upright on their bunks.

The cry is like the cry of a man dropping through space. Save me somehow! Save me! I am nothing! It is an invocation shrieked: Damn, damn your soul, be less than I, and I am something! Nigger, nigger, naught, naught, *help!*

The man cries, "Tell that woman in the cell over there she's a nigger, too!" And then he screams again.

None of us can speak. We are at the bottom of the world.

I lean against the cold steel wall, arrange my cramped limbs in a new position, and try to think, try to struggle to the surface again after that cry.

I stare at the wall across from me. A former prisoner has scratched in wide letters: FUCK THE COPS! It should really be UNFUCK THE COPS, one peacewalker has suggested; unlove them is what is meant. But a man who feels violent can imagine the act of love as an act of murder. I consider how many of the threats hurled back and forth in here take the form of coarse invitations to make love. These cries waver sometimes, in weird fashion, between the note of abuse and the note of actual flirtation, the distance between the two notes surprisingly slight. It occurs to me that I shouldn't be surprised. In each case the cry is really the same. It is: Give me your life! I hear again in my head the segregationist's hideous scream, and I think: Yes, at the heart of most violence is this delusion—that one's existence can be made more abundant by it. Just as the act of love can be imagined as murder, murder, or what amounts to it, can be imagined as an act that gives one life. It is a delusion which tantalizes us all, in one extremity or another.

Yes, the easiest way to free ourselves does always seem to be to put certain other people from us. Real or imaginary murder can be swift and apparently simple. For the moment it *is* magic, *can* set one free. It is only in time that the magic fails. In time it is proved that our lives are bound together, whether we like it or not.

I think again of this jail. The man who is cast in here—out of society—remains a member of society and in time returns, more trouble to others and to himself than he was before. The Negro, cast more violently still out of the world of people, remains a person, and the truth of this returns to trouble those who wish him a "nigger" merely, meant for service. I recall how, ironically, for those who try to believe him less than a man, this no-man tends to loom, finally, larger than life. I recall a conversation with one of the cops who has stopped in his rounds to talk with us.

We have got onto the subject of Negroes' being denied their rights. He argues for a while that their rights are not denied. "They have some advantages over us!" he suddenly asserts. "You put a prisoner who won't work into a sweat box. If he's a white man, he'll go to work after three days. A nigger can stay in there as many as thirty days!" He eyes us. "Cut a nigger and maybe he'll bleed just a little, right after you've cut, but then it'll stop. Cut a white man like that, he'll bleed to death!" He shakes his head. "A dead nigger won't begin to rot for days." He shakes his head again. "And syphilis won't drive a nigger crazy! So they have advantages *we* haven't

[27

got!" He grins. "I'm going to write to Bobby Kennedy!" I think: Your words are wild, but you are right to say that you, too, live at a disadvantage—for you are haunted. I hear again a young Negro leader addressing a mass meeting in Birmingham: "We're going to win our freedom, and as we do it, we're also going to set our white brothers free."

I remember another person who is haunted, hear again the trembling voice of a white woman two of us met while visiting influential Albany families to try to talk with them about the peace walk. She is a middle-aged woman with a face that is still pretty, but anxieties have creased and crumpled it. "We love our colored people, we love them!" she exclaims, her hand on my arm, urgent, her face peering into mine with such an entreaty that I can't help reassuring her, "Of course you do. I know." Her hand is on my arm again. "They are happy here, with things just as they are! Happy, I know it!" She begs us to leave town. "I can see that you are dedicated people, you mean well, but oh dear, you'll just do harm, you don't understand!" I ask her as gently as I can, "But if they really are happy, how can our coming make any difference?" She stares at me, confused, then just begins to shake her head.

My thoughts of her are interrupted. A cop has come into the room that opens onto the cell blocks, and the man who was yelling before begins again: "Officer! Officer!"

"What?"

"I want to talk with you!"

"What do you want? Some service?"

The man yells, "I want to get out of here!" and the cop yells back, "We all do. We're in jail, too." He gives a snort of laughter and walks off. A door slams.

The prisoner gives a great roar of frustration: "Arrrrr!

28]

It's the stinkiest dirtiest cell I was ever in!" And he lifts his steel bunk on the chain by which it is slung from the wall, then drops it, lifts it, drops it, lifts it, drops it, *clang, clang, clang.*

The Negro he has been taunting calls out, "I'm just as drunk as you are and I'm not making all that racket!"

The white man cries, "Fuck you, black bastard, I ain't fucking with you! Your ancestors were goddam slaves!" But he stops.

I think myself back into the house of the pleading woman. Sunlight pours through tall windows into the room where we sit—plays on the polished furniture, on the silky rosy-patterned rugs. She offers us, in a graceful glass dish, caramels she has made herself. Her husband is particularly fond of them, she confides; she loves to make them for him, and also to arrange the flowers. She smiles a little girl's smile. I listen for the step of servants in the large house, but hear no sound. They exist, of course; the house and the encircling garden are beautifully cared for. At the mill her husband runs, they exist too, these people whose ancestors were her ancestors' slaves, and whom, without thinking, she still calls "ours"—without thinking, but her face, as she speaks the word, dented by anxieties.

I remember the term so often used against us: We are "outside agitators." Her face before my eyes, I think: Yes, agitators, but it is above all your own doubts about your lives which we agitate; when you insist that we are out-siders, it is because, in fact, we come too close to you.

I remember the cry with which she has met the two of us at her door. At her first vague, inquiring look, we have introduced ourselves as members of the peace walk. "Oh, I'm so distressed!" she exclaims, staring at us, and her cry and her staring look draw us in an instant surprisingly near. I feel almost as though we have been recognized as relatives from out of town, appearing at a time of troubles. She leads us quickly into the house, seats us beside her on a sofa, scanning our faces. Then almost before we can begin to speak, the words leap out: "We love our colored people, love them!"

She clearly needs to have us believe it and to be able to believe it herself. She has a soft heart, has to see herself as a loving person. But clearly, too, she loves with a love that pleads: Don't make it uncomfortable for me to love you. Please don't insist on showing me all that you are, all that you feel. Let me continue to love you as my happy servants.

There pass again in my imagination Negro faces met on the road in our walk, faces of two kinds. A car approaches, goes slowly by us. A Negro family. No glance meets ours. The eyes of all are carefully veiled as they pass. On no face are feelings legible; each countenance has been drained of them as by a blow. Only a seemingly endless patience can be read there. A second car approaches. A young Negro woman is alone at the wheel. At the sight of us, black and white, and the sight of our signs, her eyes open wide, and then her whole face leaps into life, feelings written upon it like skywriting. She flings up her arms, calls out, "Well, all right then!"

The noisy prisoner is shouting again: "Shut your big black mouth. Shut your big black mouth!"

I think: The lady who offered us her caramels would turn in horror from this yelling man. And she would turn in horror from these cages which hold us; she would weep, and mean it, if she could see us in here. And yet the man yells, actually, her own desperate wish, which she cannot bear to acknowledge; and it is the daydream she dreams that holds us between these steel walls. The charge against us could be said to be that we refused to make it easier for her to live with herself.

Why are we here? We are charged with refusing to take

through Albany the one route Police Chief Laurie Pritchett told us he would allow—Oglethorpe Avenue. We
have attempted to take a route that varied from his for
five blocks and would have brought us into the business
area, where more people could read our signs. We are
here for trying this twice. Some of us tried on December
23 and served twenty-four days for it; more of us tried
again on January 27 and sit here now. After that first
arrest, the city attorney argued in court that the issue
was whether outsiders could come into Albany and tell
the police chief how to run his department. Attorney
C. B. King, who defended a few of us (others defended themselves), argued that the issue was whether
"one Laurie Pritchett" could "pit himself against the high-
est law of the land" and claim the right to deprive us of
freedom of speech. King, a local Negro, has experience of
Pritchett's claims to power, for Albany has seen wave
after wave of peaceful Negro demonstrations—or rather
has not been allowed to see them. The Chief has always
swiftly and tidily jailed the demonstrators; when the city
jail has run out of space, he has farmed them out to the
counties. At issue now—King knows, everybody knows—
is not what a handful of peacewalkers is going to do (we
would take a little more than half an hour to pass through
town and be on our way, if not arrested); it is really what
nearly half the inhabitants of Albany are going to be
allowed to do. Pritchett has been frank about it finally in
his discussions with us. Oglethorpe Avenue marks a rough
division between the city's black community and its white
community. "While I'm here, nobody is ever going to
demonstrate north of Oglethorpe." He is not even going
to let us walk down the north side of that street. "If I
let you, there'd be others." So the charge against us is
really that we challenge his right to "shut the big black
mouths" of those who want to demonstrate that they are

[31

not happy here. The city's more tenderhearted white citizens like to dream that Negro discontent does not exist, and they have delegated to Pritchett, and to the court, the power to enforce that dream.

I think of the courtroom during those early trials. I have stayed out this first time to help maintain contact between the prisoners and the outside world, and I sit there as a spectator. What childish rites are acted out as the dream is ruled to be reality! The prosecuting attorney is speaking. The court listens. Now one of my friends is speaking. It is very simple: the court stops listening. The various cops who sit up there in a line next to the judge turn to one another and begin to whisper and to laugh; the Chief and the city attorney whisper together; the Chief gets up and goes to whisper to the judge. Carl has some questions to ask the Chief. Carl is a Negro, so the Chief pretends not to be able to understand what he is saying. As Carl persists, the Chief shifts his chair so that his back is nearly turned to him. All the cops shift their chairs and laugh and yawn. Now another peacewalker is making a statement. The city attorney decides to stroll out of the room for a while. A friend of the Chief's wanders down the aisle for a brief visit with him, then wanders away again with a wave of the hand. The judge sits up there playing with the pages of a large book. If the defense rises to object to any statement by the prosecution, he swiftly overrules the objection. If the prosecution rises to object to any statement by the defense, he as swiftly honors that objection. At the conclusion of the "trial," Pritchett hands around copies of the verdict, which has been typed up in advance.

Can the truth really be manipulated as simply as this? The actors themselves appear a little self-conscious. The cops seem almost to be playing at cops. During recess, a reporter steps up to one of them to congratulate him on a promotion and the officer blushes, laughs, points at his shiny black boots: "Yes, I'm the big Gestapo now!" While the trial is in process, they sit sometimes, hands on billysticks, chins jutting—pictures of "the law." Then all at once they abandon this posture to give one another boyish punches in the stomach or to set each other's caps wrong side forward over their eyes. I half expect everyone to break out suddenly into loud guffaws and cry, "All right, all right, now let's be serious. Order in this courtroom!"

No one cries out any such thing. The absurd drama plays itself out. The absurd verdict is rendered. The prisoners are marched down to their cells, to the reality of steel walls, hard bunks, foul air, groans, curses.

Here we sit. The prisoner is yelling, "Are you in jail, are you, you black bastard? Oh, I'm glad I'm not one of you fucking niggers!"

Someone yells, "What are you in for?"

"I'm in for the hell of it!" he yells back.

Here we sit, and here I persist in thinking: The truth cannot be manipulated as simply as that. The power we have seen displayed is based on lies, and so we can prevail against it if we are stubborn. This hope has brought us here a second time. We sit and hope; we sit and stare at the steel walls and shift our cramped limbs.

FOUR

"ANYBODY dead back there yet?" Assistant Chief Friend asks cheerfully, wandering down the corridor to our cell.

"Not yet," we tell him.

He is spinning his billystick in one hand, debonair. He starts to wander off again, takes one step but changes his mind. "I fasted today, too," he informs us. "Between breakfast and lunch." He taps the bulge of midriff above his shiny belt. We congratulate him. He stares at us for a moment, then levels the stick at Edie Snyder, who sits nearest the bars, her thin feet doubled under her, jests, "I know you're eating toothpaste on the sly."

She nods. "Toothpaste and cockroaches," she replies. "And the roaches never give out."

He lingers in spite of himself, peers silently, in turn, at each one of us, crouching to find the two of us who are lying on lower bunks. "You look as though you belong in school," he says suddenly to Yvonne Klein. Yvonne is thirty years old and teaches at the University of Minnesota. He cannot really think she is a schoolgirl, but perhaps he doesn't know how to define to himself a certain look about her—bold, as the look of a schoolgirl often is, and suggesting a kind of mischief, but no threat. She lies there smiling at him strangely. Her cheeks are already deeply hollowed, her mouth is slightly open, and she keeps running her tongue across her teeth, for her gums

34]

have begun to bleed badly; fasting has given her scurvy. But even when she is sleeping, these days, there is a smile on her lips. It makes a complicated mixture of announcements, to others and perhaps to herself. It announces: I am ready for the venture. It asks: How are you going to cope with me? But it also announces: I'll do you no harm.

Assistant Chief Friend points into the next cell. (They have split up the women in the group recently, giving us two cells.) "There's the one with the evil look," he says, pointing out Kit Havice. Kit is a medical student from Colorado, very earnest. Fasting, her face has taken on an almost transparent pallor; her gray eyes sink deeper and deeper into her head. She is nearsighted and they have taken away her glasses. Her eyes shine out of her face with something of the look of a gaunt-faced newly hatched bird. Friend enacts a daily ritual with Kit. "I'd like to break this one's arm," he'll say, or, "I'd like to kick this one in the neck." She sticks her arm out through the bars, in a boyish gesture of challenge, or puts her head close, and then he grins at her. "There's the one with the evil look," he says now. Then suddenly he adds, "Well, perhaps not evil." He tells us abruptly, "You'd better all start eating," and walks off.

It is the fourteenth day most of my friends have been fasting, and for most of them it is the second time around. They have been in here before and have gone twenty-four days without food. Then they took only ten days to recover, while we negotiated again in vain for the right to walk with our signs through Albany's white business district. I look at them and breathe a question to myself: How much strength have they for this struggle?

I remember suddenly the day of their first release, remember Michele Gloor running eagerly toward the car I have brought to the back of the jail—beginning to run, but at once faltering on her sticklike legs. I run and catch hold of her as she wavers there, and she exclaims, "My legs won't run!"

"Michele, she's the pious one," Assistant Chief Friend has remarked. Another cop has said she looks like a Madonna, with her yellow hair falling to her shoulders. If he thinks her mild, he is mistaken about her. She has set for others in the group an example of how to quietly disobey orders in which she doesn't believe. In Macon most of us refused to walk into the police cars when arrested, but once booked at the station we cooperated by stepping into the paddy wagon that was to take us off to jail. Michele, to my astonishment, refused here too—though she knew that in doing so she would be on her own. She stated, "I'll walk out of a cage but not into one. People don't belong in cages." The police matron began to shout, "Bring the dog then, bring the dog!" I see Michele still, standing there, eyes wide, trembling uncontrollably but refusing to climb in. We begin to climb out of the wagon to join her and the matron suddenly changes her mind, settles the question by giving Michele a huge shove into our midst. Here in Albany a number of others followed her example and refused to walk a step after arrest.

A few refused, with her, even to walk into court. I asked them to write out their reasons and Yvonne wrote: ". . . the court, as now constituted, would be meaningless without the jail which gives it its power. But if there is anything I have learned by being in jail, it is that prisons are wrong, simply and unqualifiedly wrong . . ."

I lie remembering now the incidents of this particular struggle, that first time around, while I still watched from the outside—with a small group busy trying to communicate to the public what was happening. Chief Pritchett declared that none of the "noncooperators" would be tried until they did walk; they could go right on sitting in

36]

their cells indefinitely if they liked. He had had his men carry them into jail, but he was not going to have them carry anybody upstairs to the courtroom. He threatened first that *none* would be tried until all would agree to walk, and the day on which trial had been set, December 30, he kept them all locked up in their cages. Sitting out front in the courtroom that day, I was bewildered when no defendants entered. My friends make individual choices, and I knew that some of them—Erica Enzer, for one, among the women—felt that refusing to walk tended only to provoke officials and make it harder to communicate our point of view. The Chief whispered to the city attorney and the city attorney announced to the court that the entire group refused to appear, upon which the judge ordered them all to appear the next day and be tried for contempt. The next day Erica and several of the men cleared themselves of this charge; they climbed the stairs to testify that they had been as willing to appear the day before. The Chief did not try to prevent this; he was not at all embarrassed by the fact that it was plain now that he had asked the city attorney to announce a lie the day before. And it did not occur to the court that he should be embarrassed—the judge asked him no questions about it. The five defendants who did in fact refuse to walk were given seven days for contempt, and a week later, when the others were tried on the main charges, they were given another seven days.

I think of Erica, the day of that trial. Erica does not choose Michele's way to be stubborn, but she chooses her own, which has as often taken me by surprise. I hear her again in court, delivering her own defense, logical, precise, A, B, C, D. If she had refused to walk, she would not have been able to confront them with her argument. The opposition, of course, simply pretends not to be able to understand her: she was born in Czechoslovakia and though she has lived in this country for years (she is a lab technician in Chicago) she still has an accent. I see her summoning her bold words. I see her, too, as she approaches the courtroom that day. A short, stout woman in her late thirties, she is flushed from mounting the steep stairs. The fast is marking her already, has chopped flesh from her cheeks, allowed her cotton skirt to sag. I stare at her, wondering for a moment whether the spirit in her has been thinned. As she moves toward the courtroom, we hear a guard inform a Negro couple that the trial will be closed to the public. As though a spring has been touched, the motion instantaneous, I see Erica's eyes open wide, her chin thrust itself forward, her entire being thrust itself forward. Her words jump from her: "They can't do this!" The others in the group then join the protest, insisting that the Chief has promised an open trial; and he does finally have the doors opened—after a number of Negroes from the town, come to show support, have accepted the guard's words and left.

The people tried that day were given twenty-five days, unless they would pay fines—which none of them would. With credit for eighteen days served already, that left them seven more days. But I began to wonder how long those who refused to walk would have to endure before release. Yvonne grew sicker than the rest, and the Chief ordered her taken to the hospital. He also gave instructions that there should be no force-feeding; she was not to be fed until she asked to be. I caught a glimpse of her in the hospital corridor as she was wheeled past (she was to have no visitors; this was jail still), and she called out that she was not going to ask—she would eat when they set her free. I was told that if I was worried about her and Allen Cooper, whom they had also brought to the hospital, I could get a court order instructing the doctor to feed them; or, of course, I could pay their fines.

These possibilities tormented me as the days passed, although I knew that they were inconsistent with the spirit in which my friends were fasting. I began to despair of the Chief's relenting. My hopelessness deepened when Ray Robinson decided to increase his protest and stop taking water as well as food. (He sent a note out: "I'm willing to see just how much they really hate me. Yes, I'm willing to find out . . .") I put through a call to one of my brothers, who is a doctor, and asked him how long Ray could live if nothing were done for him. My brother told me he could live a week at the most; he *could* die within a matter of hours—everything depended on his condition. Ray had great stamina, I knew, for he had once been a prize fighter, but he had gone many days without food, and he lay in a cell even more crowded and stifling than the others. We alerted friends of the project, who sent wires and telephoned to Pritchett and to the city doctor, expressing their concern; but I began to wonder whether the Chief would even have him taken to the hospital for observation. "The nigger's tough," the cops remarked. "*He* won't die." One of the men sent a note out to us reporting that Ray lay in his cell groaning. I felt panic. The Negro attorney, C. B. King, had been visiting the jail, because he had as clients two of the men in our group, who planned to appeal their cases; he also knew Albany. I called him and asked him whether he thought the authorities were capable of just letting Ray die. He told me, "If they don't move by tomorrow, I'm going to take it on myself to have his fine paid and get him out of there." I said, "Ray would want me to tell you not to." But then I added helplessly, "I can't help being glad that you will."

In the morning he called back with news: Ray had been taken to the hospital at last and was being fed intravenously; so were Yvonne and Allen. The city itself had obtained the court order. I put down the phone as one of the office group walked into the room and I tried to tell her the news, but I was crying so that I couldn't; she looked at me in terror, sure that the news was that someone was dead. I remind myself now: it was after I had given up hope that it happened.

Pritchett had decided after all to force-feed the prisoners, but unless he also changed his mind about having them carried into court, all of the noncooperators would soon be in Yvonne's condition, and I wondered for how many days they could hold up under forced feeding.

A number of supporters had turned up, meanwhile, from various parts of the country, and they had stood out in front of the jail, fasting too, to demonstrate their concern. Pritchett had arrested all of them. He had let some of them stand out there for a number of hours during a heavy rainstorm, but as soon as the rain stopped, he had made the arrest. On the morning of January 15 I turned up for the trial of these six, and suddenly word spread that the noncooperators would be carried to court to be tried as well.

I stood with my face pressed to the glass of the courthouse front door. No one was to be let in while the defendants were being taken upstairs, but the stairs were straight across the hall there, and at the foot of the stairs was the door to the jail. Three supporters were refusing to walk, too. The men were dragged by the cops. I saw Eric Robinson going up, looking very small—dragged shoulders first, white-trousered legs knocking against the steps. One of his shoes fell off and remained on a step. Two cops dragged John-i-thin Stephens, taking him up feet first. His long thin body sagged between them. He tried to hold himself so that he wouldn't be bumped, but I saw his hands, clasped around the back of the cop who had him by the shoulders, slide. Some Negro work-crew prisoners had been ordered to carry up the woman. Yvonne had been brought back from the hospital, and they carried her past on a stretcher. She lifted her head and then waved. One of them came out of the door carrying Edie in his arms. He carried her gingerly, ill at ease, and she was trying to hold herself so as to make it easier for him. Her clothes seemed to fit her strangely. I stared at her. Edie was one of the liveliest among us, full of wit, talkative, venturesome—a thin black-haired girl from Brooklyn who had been A. J. Muste's secretary. She looked hushed and small. The trusty began to mount the stairs with her, very slowly. I watched, hypnotized. My face pressed against the glass, I thought: How frail all of you are, and bedraggled. Some of the white people who worked in the building stood in a corner, laughing. But another thought, too, held me rooted there: the Chief was giving the order he had declared he never would give. The two thoughts joined strangely. I recognized: I am watching actually a show of strength. I remind myself now that those who were being dragged and carried that day and seemed awkward and vulnerable were gaining there a part at least of what they had been struggling for. In court the five who had refused to walk and the supporters who had joined us were given thirty-one days, with thirty of those days suspended—which meant that the city wanted to be rid of us and had decided to release all imprisoned walkers the next day.

One prisoner is yelling to another: "Do you want me to whip your ass? You come around here and I'll whip your ass!"

The second prisoner is yelling back: "Shut up shut up shut up shut up!"

I muse on our contest with the city—muse on the subject of our strength and the strength of those who now hold us here again. I remember our partial victory and ask

[41

myself how much I can read into it. The Chief had done that day what he had sworn he would never do; but then the Chief is not a man to be embarrassed particularly about the breaking of his word. He had not, after all, given way to us on the main point and allowed us to walk in the downtown area of Albany.

A woman who has been put in the cell next to us—with Kit and Michele and Mary and Candy—yells in a voice hoarse with drink: "Peter Natchez, are you in there?"

Peter Natchez answers from a distant cell, "Baby, you know I'm here."

She yells to him, "How long you been in here, baby? Come here!"

He answers, "Sugar, I can't come there."

I wonder: How much strength do we actually have to move the authorities if we hang on? And how much strength do we have to hang on?

The woman yells, "Peter, I said come here!"

I lie flat on my back, musing a little feverishly. For the last few days I have been sick, and today is the first day I have felt well enough again to ask myself questions about anything but my own strength. Before coming into jail I told my friends that I could not fast with them; I was afraid that, if I did, I might come out with my health wrecked, for experience had taught me that after a few days of fasting I collapsed. They wanted me with them anyway and, once in, I decided that I could safely go on a partial fast—eating part of one of the two meals served each day—and so keep them a kind of company. But I misjudged. After nine days, when we were called to trial, I was startled to find how hard it was to climb the stairs to court, and once in the courtroom itself, I sat struggling not to faint. It was after the trial that four of us were moved from the crowded women's cell into a second, adjoining cell. The next morning, when a guard brought us mattress covers and I began to pull mine on, I suddenly felt my heart begin to stammer and all my remaining strength explode and give way. The city doctor turned up later in the day. He was visiting every day now, at Pritchett's orders. He would ask us to stick out our tongues. That was all the examination, but he was giving the fasters vitamin shots (since most of them did not feel they should take vitamins voluntarily). When my friends told him that I was sick, he treated the news with suspicion. He was suspicious of us all. He gave me a vitamin pill, but when they asked him to examine me, he declined. It frightened me not to know my real condition. I was feeling steadily worse, and the next day I had a brief convulsion. (The doctor treated the report of this, too, with skepticism.) After some anguish of mind, I decided to accept the orange juice which Chief Pritchett brought me when he saw how I looked, and I began that next day to eat part of breakfast as well as dinner. For several days now I have lain in a partial swoon, too weak even to wash myself, feeling my strength, at times, drain from me so utterly that I had to fight off a dread of dying; but now for the first day I feel within myself a fragile equilibrium. Relieved from concentration upon myself, I look about at my friends and try to imagine the days ahead for them.

All of them have shown a physical stamina that amazes me. Most of them are half my age, in their twenties or even younger. But each of them faces, in time, the kind of physical collapse I have just experienced, and dread of death, should the doctor be careless, or confused, about them too.

Edie jumps to her knees on the upper bunk, where she has been turning the pages of a newspaper. "Friends— Strawberry Bavarian Cream. 1 package frozen strawberries, 2 envelopes gelatin, ¼ cup cold water or milk, ¼ cup sugar, 2 eggs, 1 heaping cup crushed ice, 1 cup cream.

Defrost berries and heat a half cup juice to simmer . . ."
Yvonne leans her head back against the steel cell wall
(scrawled with LINDA HASTY AND DAVID HUGGINS, "SUPER"
NORMON, BEATRICE I LOVE YOU). She claps her hands together silently. We have discovered, to our surprise, that
it helps to talk about food, and we do so endlessly.

The woman in the next cell is yelling again: "I said
come here, Peter! I said come here!"

Yvonne climbs down from her top bunk to get a drink.
Suddenly she puts her head down on Edie's bunk, holding to the mattress. Her legs waver under her as though
they were rubber, then straighten. She lifts her head
again. Edie asks her, "What color spots do you see today?" Everybody has begun to have dizzy spells. Yvonne
fishes Turgenev's *A Sportsman's Sketches* from under the
lower bunk and climbs back up to her perch.

Watching her with anxiety, I recall in sharp detail the
doctor's visit on the day I first felt frightened for myself.
When he handed me a vitamin pill, I felt too weak to
take the step across the cell to the faucet for a drink to
help me swallow it. I said that I would take it later. He
stiffened, suspicious, and said, "I want to *see* you take it."
I told him that he could trust me to take it, but he repeated, "Let me see you take it now." So I stood up and
filled a paper cup with water, put the pill in my mouth
and took a drink, and then I suddenly felt so badly that
I flopped down on my bunk on my stomach: "See if she's
taken it," he ordered Pritchett's secretary, Mrs. Anderson, who assists him on his visits. She stooped down and
decided that I wasn't holding the pill in my mouth and
then they both left the cell.

I turned over on my back. I wanted to sit up again but
I had no strength to do it. I was frightened. The center
of my being seemed to be vanishing; I felt my cheeks collapse as though I were a space pilot going through some

44]

peculiar experiment. Yvonne stared at me and exclaimed, "You look awful!" She called after the doctor, "Could you examine Barbara? She looks awful." The doctor walked back to the door of our cell. He said, "She should expect to feel awful." And then in a trembling voice, "I don't know whether you're Communists or whether you're all crazy, but you're not Americans!" And then he walked away.

I lay very quiet. He was a doctor; I was sick and frightened; but he was walking away. Sobriety entered me like a chill. Yes, we were in jail—those who have been cast out. I was one of them now, and my friends were. Now I knew how great a distance lay between us and others.

I think: As my friends fall sick, their lives will be in the hands of this man who has walked away. I think of how many days there are for them to survive. Most of us have been sentenced to thirty days, with no time suspended this round because of time served before trial—and so, twenty-six more days. Others, who had had some days after trial suspended the last time, have been given ten extra days for violation of probation. A few people have not even been tried yet and face an indefinite stay. These again are the noncooperators. This time the Chief, without a word, had his men carry them up to court, but the men, without thinking, set them down not at the front of the courtroom, as before, but far to the back. When the judge called for Candy Kricker and Mary Suzuki to step forward, they stated that they couldn't, and the judge, surprised and irritated, ordered them back to their cells. Nobody was carried up on the second day of trial, and so, among the women, Candy, Mary, Michele and Kit have not been tried.

Nor has Yvonne, although on the second day of trial she chose to walk. When a cop carried her the first day— half dragging her, an arm about her waist, her blouse hitched up and her ribs showing, her face drawn and ashen—it was so painful for her that she decided she could not go through it again and stated that she would walk, reluctantly. In spite of this, the judge, after some whispered exchanges with the Chief, decided to postpone her trial too—until everybody would walk. Now I am worried about her especially.

She was the first to fall sick the last time, and this time she has been fasting longer than anyone else—eighteen days already—because she came in four days earlier. On January 23 she and a local S.N.C.C. worker, Phil Davis, decided to picket a civil-defense exercise in town. The paper announced that a group of people would spend twenty-four hours underground, "simulating wartime conditions," to prove that they could be endured; they would even pretend quarrels among themselves, to make the experience more "real." Yvonne and Phil decided to pass out leaflets on the spot, pointing out the test's absurdity. They were arrested within fifteen minutes.

"What law did they break?" we asked Assistant Chief Friend, who made the arrest, when he came around one day. Peaceful picketing is supposed to be any citizen's right.

They disobeyed his order to leave, he told us calmly.

We asked him, "If the cop is the law, doesn't that make Albany a police state?"

He shrugged, confused. "You were loitering!" he decided. When we laughed at this, he grinned himself.

I can worry a little less about some of my friends, because they were arrested a week later than most of us, so they have been fasting a week less. A week after seventeen of us tried to resume the Walk through Albany's white downtown area, nine others tried to picket at Turner Air Force Base. We had made a point of demonstrating at military installations throughout the Walk. Pritchett warned that he did not give permission for this, either; but we had never been arrested for picketing at a base anywhere in the United States—as we told him; so we were not absolutely sure that he would make this arrest. The demonstrators dressed for jail, nevertheless—pulled on two shirts or two blouses, two sets of underwear. Early that morning those of us already in jail heard the clatter of steel stretchers lifted down from their racks, and we knew the Chief was going to show us again that he *was* Chief. Not long after, we heard Bradford Lyttle's clear shout ringing through the jail: "Friends! How are you all?" We shouted back. Candy Kricker was dragged down the corridor to our cell, looking a little startled. She sat on the floor, small, plump, disheveled, rubbing her bruises. And just before her, Mary Suzuki was dragged to our door—a Canadian student whom we had heard about but had never seen, a new supporter turned up to join our battle. This was her first trip to jail and her first fast. She looked frail enough already, a slender girl with a delicate pensive face and dressed not in the usual jail-going clothes but in silk stockings, pretty shoes, an elegant maroon-colored coat. A cop dragged her to our door by the collar of her coat, and she lay on the cement floor, among the cigarette butts, while he hunted for the key to our cell, smiling up at us with a look expectant, almost happy, extraordinarily mild—as though she had just arrived at the new world not of a jail cell but of some pleasant island. Soon after we had introduced ourselves and exchanged a few words, she curled up at the end of one bunk and abruptly fell asleep. I hear her now, talking to the drunken woman who has been yelling shrilly. She is suggesting to her, in a voice so soft and weary that I can hardly hear her, that Peter Natchez, in the distant cell, really can't come here. The woman goes on yelling.

Another friend has joined us without meaning to. Eric Robinson had volunteered to stay out of jail this time and be one of those who worked to keep us in touch with the outside world. On the day of the arrests at the base, he went to the courthouse to find out what Pritchett had decided to say were the charges against the new prisoners. With him was Dr. Arthur Samuels of Dartmouth Medical School, who had come down for a few days to be of what help he could. Samuels did most of the talking. When he asked what the charges were, Pritchett told them both to get out. Samuels asked if they could see him later, then, and introduced himself. The Chief replied that he didn't care whether Samuels was Khrushchev himself—to get out. They got out, the Chief following closely. "I think his blood pressure must have been something like three hundred," Samuels testified at Eric's trial. As Eric was backing out the door, he too asked if Pritchett could just tell them the charges, and as they were descending the front steps, he turned again and asked, "May I see you later, then?" The Chief's anger exploded. He called to one of his cops, "Arrest him!" And as the professor, amazed, hurried off down the street —seeing another cop coming toward *him*—Eric was dragged back up the steps and into jail with the rest of us. We heard the men in the other cell block crying out his name.

He was given forty days. The prosecution charged, especially, that he had pointed his finger at the Chief—a "challenging" gesture. A witness for the city declared, "If you point your finger at somebody, you're usually looking for trouble." Eric is a twenty-year-old artist from California, very slight in build, with tight curly blond hair, eyes set like sparks in flat cheeks rather like an Eskimo's, and a curly mouth like a cherub's—a frail David to the Chief's Goliath. Actually, both Eric and Samuels testified that he had not even pointed his finger; he had raised his hand in a gesture familiar to all of us: all right, then, goodbye. The judge summed up: "There has been evidence given on both sides, and it is hard for me to determine the truth, so I find you guilty."

I hear Kit, in the next cell, trying to reason with the drunken woman. Everybody's tired, she suggests, and some people aren't well. Couldn't she perhaps be quiet for a little while and let them rest, and get a little rest herself? The woman exclaims, "You can't ask a Christian to be quiet!" and goes on yelling. Yvonne, in the bunk across from me, suddenly puts her book down and draws the coat she has been using as a blanket up over her head.

I think of my friends, growing frailer every day, and of all the days that stretch ahead of them. And I think of the kind of power against which we are pitted, the license those opposed to us feel to do with us pretty much as they wish—in the name of "law and order." I muse on that elastic "law," which lets them arrest Eric for asking a question, postpone Yvonne's trial in order to put pressure on her friends, ignore the law of the land. We carry with us a letter from the American Civil Liberties Union, citing Supreme Court decisions about one's right to carry out the kind of peaceful demonstrations for which we have been arrested here. "You're not in Supreme Court country now," one man we have met along the road has remarked to us. And we are in country where the stranger is guilty until he proves himself innocent.

We all share Eric's "guilt." They imagined that he had pointed a judging finger. This really is the charge against us all. I remember the city attorney, huge Grady Rawls, and his courtroom tirades against us: "You prowl our streets, without respect for anyone or anything!" His heavy cheeks tremble as he speaks; the fat cigar trembles in his hand. And I remember one of the cops who has lingered in the corridor outside our cell to question us. "You were never headed for Cuba!" he suddenly accuses. "You were headed for Albany from the start!" For a moment we think he is joking, but plainly he is not. His cheek, too, trembles. He really does see us setting out from Quebec, over two thousand miles away, our single-minded purpose to harass the city of Albany.

They act with the license of people convinced that they are under assault. Their courtroom is not in reality a court of law; it is a kind of outpost which they man against their enemies. This is why the chief of police directs proceedings there. He directs, as they see it, the defensive.

And all's fair in a war of defense. I recall the tactics used against Ray. He had decided to go on another water fast at the start of this second jail term. This time the Chief moved quickly: he began proceedings to have him committed to an asylum. He asked us with a big grin, "Do you know where they've taken Ray?" He had him taken first to the psychiatric ward, for observation—the city doctor concurring in the move. Frightened, Ray broke his fast. The Chief then had photographs of him eating and passed them around among us. "And he's getting out now; he thinks you've lost faith in him," he told us—staring one of us, then another, very straight in the eye, as he liked to do when he was lying. We told him, "We know he doesn't think that, Chief." We questioned him then about the suspicions he had that Ray might be crazy. "I never thought he was," the Chief told us blandly. "You have to use psychology sometimes."

I think about this man who is the figure at the gate of the city, Albany's defender. A big redheaded man with a bull's heavy-barreled chest and a bull's heavy shoulders, small blue eyes that move quickly—his very physical presence communicates stubbornness and a touchy pride. I

50]

remember an interview I had with him in his office during the first jail-in—to ask whether he would not allow me to visit the prisoners. He had canceled visiting privileges after some of them refused to walk to court. C. B. King, able to visit as a lawyer, had misunderstood Kit to say that she was too weak to walk, and I was worried. (When she told him that she couldn't walk, she really meant on principle.) Pritchett said to me, "Nobody's too weak to walk," and he told me no, I could not visit. Something moved him to declare then, "I fasted once for six months and I had no trouble walking." The ring of the telephone interrupted his strange boast. A newspaper reporter was at the other end of the line; the conversation was about us, and before he hung up, Pritchett raised his voice and stated: "We'll just wait and see who lasts the longest." I decided not to question him about his own "fast." Had he perhaps gone on a diet? I never learned. I asked him whether any doctor was checking on the prisoners' condition. He told me, "They don't need a doctor." He stared at me, and then declared, "*They're* eating." I said, "I don't believe that's so, Chief."

His brow abruptly lowered; his face flushed fiery red; he rose from behind his large flat-topped desk—the Confederate flag displayed behind it—and strode to the door, throwing it open for me. (By the side of the door was a large photograph of his cops lined up in battle array.) I felt he wanted to hit me and was controlling himself with effort. I remembered the story I had heard of how he had dragged a Negro girl through the jail by her hair. I forget our final words. I tried to appear calm. From then on—during the period in which I was outside the jail—whenever we met on the City Hall steps or in the hall, though I would say "Good morning, Chief," and try to catch his eye, he would stare through me or past me, pretending not to see that I was there.

Yes, I think, a violent man, who experiences even more strongly than most of us the impulse simply to deny existence to whatever disturbs him; one, too, who knows that he has been delegated to obey just this impulse, whenever he can manage, for "everybody's good." One who has managed many times—has put troublesome men behind bars, denied troublesome truths by lies—and who feels his strength.

I ask myself: Are there any in this city who will question his actions, or who will perhaps begin to question them if we persist? Then I recall the recent visit paid us by a local minister. The Chief has decided again to curtail our visiting privileges—though he restored them after a while the last time—and only lawyers or ministers can see us. This day a chaplain from the air base suddenly appeared. He knew friends of Kit's parents and came to speak particularly with her. He was a slim, smiling young man with scrubbed pale face, with pale-rimmed glasses. Kit lay on a lower bunk, so he crouched there in the corridor to be close to her, but he was careful not to let his neatly pressed trousers actually touch the floor. He peered at her and I saw his face change, as though it had been lightly struck. He drew a breath and managed to declare, "Well, you certainly look grand!"

He stared again for a moment, making himself smile; then he asked her whether any of us had been treated brutally. She told him no. He asked eagerly, "Then am I correct in saying that any privations you are suffering are of your own choice?" Kit told him that we thought the arrests unjust; we didn't choose to be jailed, though we had been prepared to be. The young minister crouched there, silent for a moment. Then he said, "This isn't said as a threat, of course, but I hope you realize that the authorities here are most rigid?"

Kit laughed and said yes, we had received that impression. He began to talk now about Albany's race relations: he had lived there as a child, but then moved away; when he had returned he'd seen such a difference! He thought the air base had a lot to do with it. Kit moved eagerly into a discussion of war and peace and what she understood to be the pacifist message of Christianity. He looked surprised and argued the point: it was sometimes necessary to give one's life for one's country. She asked him if the issue wasn't one of *taking* lives. He soon changed the subject by presenting her with a Bible. Then he began to urge her to break her fast: Jesus said, "Thou shalt love thy neighbor as thyself," which clearly implied that one should love oneself. Kit reminded him that he had just said it was sometimes necessary to offer one's life. He stared at her again, and again I saw his face change—become rather helplessly sober and puzzled. He found his smile again, and he repeated his words as though Kit had not spoken. He said brightly, "I leave you with that thought," and left.

Now I remember his words: "This isn't said as a threat, of course, but I hope you realize that the authorities . . ." The man of God backing up the policeman. I think: Why do we hope to move anyone in this town? Then I remember the look of surprise that I have seen touch his face for a moment like a light blow. Perhaps we *can* hope.

I have seen this surprise even on the face of Laurie Pritchett. He visits our cell almost every day. Some days he comes to try a little "psychology"—to suggest that he may separate us from each other, move us all to different county jails; or to tell us that A. J. Muste has wired that he wants to pay our fines and get us out; or perhaps to report that Bradford Lyttle, the Walk's coordinator, whom he *has* isolated from the rest of us, in the county jail across the street, has broken fast—"You should have

[53

seen him putting down that big steak!" (We had been afraid that his first "news" might be so, but the next two reports caused much laughter—especially the news of Brad's meal, for he is a vegetarian.) Sometimes the Chief comes, it seems, just out of curiosity, either by himself or to listen to our conversations with C. B. King. Edie likes to tease him lightly. She calls him the hotelkeeper, and he smiles at this. One day when he was standing there outside our cell, next to C. B. King, C. B. asked if we had any messages to send out, and Edie answered flamboyantly, "Much, much love to everybody!"

C. B. said he wouldn't carry such generalized love; surely there were some people out there we didn't mean to send it to.

Edie laughed but—looking toward Pritchett—answered that we wouldn't really begrudge it to anybody. She said, "I think we even love our keepers."

C. B. raised his eyebrows at that and smiled a subtle bitter smile: he didn't love them. I glanced at Pritchett. He stood staring at Edie—or not so much at Edie as at the words she had spoken—and for a moment I saw his face relax in astonishment. It quite altered his look, which was, for that long moment, almost boyishly pensive and vulnerable.

And at other moments his hostility toward us has dropped. During the first jail-in I heard that Pritchett had said, "I wish Barbara would come into jail and stop putting out all those lies." I wrote him a letter, saying that it troubled me that he imagined we published lies; I would send him a complete file of the press releases I wrote, and I hoped that he would correct any mistakes he found in them. After the first sentences had been served, I went with Brad Lyttle and with Ralph Di Gia to negotiate with Pritchett and with City Manager Stephen Roos about continuing the Walk. Mr. Roos was very defensive

54]

and began by complaining that we had falsely reported that the cops here had used cattle prods against us. I turned to the Chief and, not at all certain what his response would be, asked him to assure Roos that we had issued no such statement. He did, quite gravely.

He was wary with us that day, and of course he did not give the permission that we wanted, but as he joked clumsily with Brad about the weight the fasters had lost, it struck me that he didn't hide a certain puzzled respect for them. Brad told me that after the first trial, at which Brad made a long statement, Pritchett visited his cell and seemed "a different man," curious about us and eager to talk. Turning up after my own recent court statement, he astonished me by saying, "You made a good speech."

I hear, in imagination, the chiding voices of skeptical friends back home: "No! You're not really hoping that you can melt this cop's heart finally—make such a 'different man' out of him, by your nonviolent ways, that he will hand you the key to the city in an impulsive gesture!"

In a distant cell a woman begins to laugh hysterically. "Heh, heh, baby!" somebody calls.

No, we do not hope to convert Chief Laurie Pritchett.

A letter has come just today from one of my friends, begging us to give up the battle. This second series of arrests has distressed her: "I think you are being wasteful of time, energy, health . . . You are exceeding your mark . . . You have exhausted your *persuasions* (Pritchett has listened to you, and answered no), and you are now *forcing* them to arrest you, since their minds remain unchanged. . . . The position they have taken all their lives toward what you represent must either be cracked by total conversion (which is more and more out of the question) or—and this I think you ignore like ostriches—find itself *reinforced*. . . . I would have preferred that you move around the obstacle, go your way, walk your walk, deliver your messages. 'To yield,' says Lao-tse, 'is to be preserved whole.' "

I begin to compose a letter to her in my head. We do not hope for anybody's "total conversion." But I shall try to say to her what we do hope.

FIVE

D^{EAR} ———,
I'm sorry that you are distressed by our actions.
I'll try to explain what it is that we think we are doing.
It is early morning and the yelling back and forth between
cells has stopped for a time; all is very quiet. If it will
only stay quiet for a little while . . .

You'll excuse my writing on toilet paper. At least it un-
winds nicely, like a scroll.

But now I have sat here for I'm not sure how long,
not writing at all, just enjoying the luxury of this silence.
It is so rare in here that, when it occurs, it's an almost
intoxicating pleasure.

This, of course, brings me back to your question: What
are we doing here? Why don't we pay our fines and get
out? You feel that we have exhausted persuasion—which
is the means proper to nonviolent struggle—and by insisting still on trying to have our way, we begin to do a kind
of violence both to ourselves and to our antagonists: We
are *bound* to be hurt now, and they are *bound* to have to
hurt us; we force them to.

But we have not begun to exhaust persuasion. I'm not
sure that we are going to win. But it is not blind of us to
hope still; it would be blind to give up hope so soon.

We place our hopes in a very particular kind of persuasion, and I don't think you have ever really understood the nature of it. I have never made it clear. And so
you ascribe to us the most naïve of hopes. In your letter

[57

you try to make me see that we cannot really expect to accomplish a total conversion of our opponents; they are not going to "sit down and reflect mildly on the doctrines of love which have been poured in their ears by twenty-six young strangers." You picture us to yourself as hoping to touch the hearts of our opponents in a very simple and melodramatic way. Isn't this your vision of a nonviolent siege? You see us standing before Chief Pritchett and declaring to him that we think he is being unjust; we are careful not to raise our voices or to clench our fists; we stand there showing ourselves to be the most endearing people, full of love and goodwill. And—hopefully—suddenly—his heart cracks. A small voice inside him cries, "Brothers! I used to be like you when I was a little boy! Teach me to be that way again!"

No wonder nonviolence seems to you no answer to the world's great and complicated problems. I have heard you argue that few people would be able to practice it, and few would be likely to respond. No wonder that you think so.

Every now and then something has happened on this Walk that has borne a remote resemblance to the caricature you hold in your mind. Confronted by people who were treating us as though we were not human, one of us has managed, by a look or a word or a gesture, to assert: I *am* human; treat me as though I were—and has succeeded in making the other do just that.

One day back in October, for example, we were walking single-file through Klan country near Athens, Georgia, and as Yvonne Klein crossed the yard of a small country store, the proprietor came out, screaming threats, his face convulsed. I was walking a little way behind her, and I saw him grab her by the neck. She managed to remain very calm. I saw her turn, slow-motion, and look him quietly in the face; and he dropped his hands. When I caught up with her a little later, she told me that he had had a knife pressed to her shoulder.

Later that day several members of the Klan drove by in a sound truck—four stout middle-aged men in sheets and peaked hats, riding in back, two younger men up front with a microphone. On the mike they were "calling all white men, calling all white men" to attend a rally that night to discuss what to do about us. One member of the Walk at the time was Tom Rodd, a small tousle-headed young man of seventeen who looked even younger. You would probably have laughed at the sight of him—or shaken your head. He had bought a child's tin horn at the five-and-ten and wore it slung at his belt in a little felt scabbard he had sewn, and he liked to rally the walkers after rest periods with reveilles upon it. It served rather well, as a matter of fact—both to bring us to our feet and to lighten our spirits a little. We could become too solemn. But he did look like a figure out of a fairy tale—the youngest son with his magic horn and his hero's faith that it was all he needed. When the truck slowed down and drew alongside us, the white-robed men scowled at us and Tom stared back at them, his eyes wide, and suddenly singling out one of them—who had a big cigar jammed between his teeth—he cried out in his slight, boyish voice: "Peace be with you, sir!" The man took the cigar out of his mouth and replied in a pompous solemn voice, before he could think what he was doing, "Peace be with *you!*" A moment later, of course, he did think. At the next driveway the truck turned around and returned, and as it passed us now the man up front was screaming over the microphone: "They talk of peace, but the Bible says there *is* no peace, there *is* no peace!" It was a little hard for them to recover the initiative, though, and they drove off. Tom told me later, by the way, "My immediate inclination was to say something

[59

like, 'Hey, fat 'n' funky, whyn'cha take a bath?' But other impulses prevailed." It is not that any of us are walking saints; we simply observe a certain discipline.

You probably read the report in *Liberation* of what happened to the walkers in Griffin, Georgia, the day they refused to cooperate with what they felt to be an unjust arrest and the cops tried to make them walk—first into the nearby jail, then upstairs to their cells—by torturing them with an electric cattle prod. I wasn't there, as you know; I had gone north for a few days. When my friends just took the torture and continued to refuse to walk, all but one of the cops began to feel ashamed, and finally only one man was using the prodder; but he used it savagely and obscenely. Do you remember that two cops, though they did nothing to stop him, began to cry, in spite of themselves? But one moment was described to me that is the particular reason for my recalling the day to you. Once they had been booked, a few of my friends did walk upstairs, but most refused and were carried or dragged very roughly. Eric Robinson was the last to be booked. He was asked by the cops, "Are you going to walk?" He answered that he wouldn't. Eric is about Tom's size and, like Tom, has an almost child's-storybook look about him. He said very quietly, and as though he could believe that they would do what he asked, "Please be careful with me." And to everybody's astonishment, he was carried upstairs very carefully.

Moments like this are the magic moments in a project like ours. And the magic is not a matter of illusion. The extent to which one can affect how others will behave simply by looking for one kind of behavior rather than another—well, who knows the extent? It deserves endless study. I know that I have sometimes felt the power of it to an almost intoxicating degree. I have felt it when we walked up to groups of young toughs along the road—

60]

youths who had driven past in their cars and parked to wait for us, clearly hungering for violence; and simply by walking up to them in a friendly way, as though we feared nothing from them, we have been able—well, to bewilder them out of attacking. The Quakers would call it "speaking to that of God in another man." It is not a matter of naïveté, as you seem to suspect. The discipline required is analogous to an actor's discipline. Just as an actor can train himself to believe in the events of a play, and through his act of belief he makes the play real to an audience (and sometimes also to other less experienced actors), so we try to control our fear and to believe in the possibility that our antagonist will behave as though he recognized a human bond between us; and that belief—when we can find it—has an hypnotic quality.

But I had better say rapidly, before you begin to misunderstand me again, that yes, one can expect much too much of such "magic." One can expect too much of oneself, and forget how suddenly belief can fail one. Or one can expect *always* to be able to inhibit violent action in others if one is in control of oneself; and this would be absurd. As you know, we *have* been attacked. Above all, in a situation like our present one, if we hoped to bring about a change in an entire city's policy simply through holding the thought that the change could come—well, we would be lunatics.

There is a very beautiful passage in Proverbs: "As in water face answereth to face, so the heart of man to man." It often does, especially when people act on the assumption that it can; but if it always did, we would have the Kingdom of God on earth. I feel that I have to assure you that we don't believe the Kingdom has come. We do know that men are quite able to look straight at other men and deny to themselves that they are human. To bring others to acknowledge our humanity and treat us

[61

accordingly—with justice—we have usually to resort to more than friendliness. We have to rely on *a kind of force* —which I'll try to define and to distinguish from violence.

You chide in your letter that we are now "entering on active behavior" and it looks violent to you; "it cannot any longer be called passive resistance." I'm glad you introduced that term so that I can say I wish it had never been used to describe this kind of struggle. It describes in a literal way, of course, certain tactics, such as "going limp." But it has always been misunderstood to mean that our basic attitude is passive. The word coupled with "passive" is forgotten—"resistance." It is also too bad that "nonviolent action" describes merely what our actions are *not*; and in this term the word "action" is forgotten. We have not suddenly "entered on active behavior"; we have put our faith in it from the beginning. We believe in the power of nonviolent acts to speak louder than words.

All the way along the route, of course, we have tried words first. I have meant for a long time to write you about the extraordinary interviews we have had with police officials. Before we enter a town, two or three of us always pay an advance visit to the chief of police or the sheriff, sometimes also to the mayor. We don't want to take them by surprise. Even before this visit we mail them information about the walk. We explain that we don't come to ask for protection, but simply to let them know our plans, so as to give them the minimum of trouble in regulating traffic as we pass through. We specifically do not ask for permission, for we are within our constitutional rights; we just describe to them what we will be doing. But of course—Constitution or no—many places, especially in the South, have local ordinances that forbid or drastically limit "parading" or passing out leaflets. We have been promptly informed of this, time after time. We have managed to walk through anyway, and obtained our rights just by talking.

This is the way it would go: The chief of police (it usually was) would declare bluntly that we weren't going to walk through, and that was that. Or perhaps that we could walk through all right, but it couldn't be on the main street, and we couldn't pass out any leaflets. One of us would start talking then, careful to stop to listen whenever the chief opened his mouth, but quietly drawing this picture for him: (1) We had already walked through any number of towns, all the way from Quebec—without trouble. (2) We hoped to have and give no trouble here, and to be through the town and on our way in a matter of minutes. (3) Though we hoped for no trouble, we were all quite ready to go to jail if we had to; we had been there before. The person talking would not belabor the subject of constitutional rights and Supreme Court decisions confirming them, knowing how Southerners tend to feel about Supreme Court decisions; but the advance mailing we send always includes a letter the American Civil Liberties Union has sent us on the subject. He would also be careful to make clear our respect for the chief's *proper* authority—by asking various questions about traffic rules. He would talk slowly, letting the chief weigh all this.

I was present at a number of these encounters, and almost always as the talks began I would think to myself: This time it is not going to work; this chief won't budge. He would be a big loud-voiced red-faced man, or a lean wrinkled one with a hard shining eye, and he'd say, "Well, I'm not going to allow that in this town—hear?" And I'd think: No, he is not. Tom Rodd would be doing the talking for us, or perhaps John-i-thin Stephens, with his long dreamy face, his look of someone just emerging from sleep, very slow in all his motions, the long cuffs of

[63

his sweater almost hiding his hands as he gestured—and a voice so quiet you could sometimes hardly hear it. I would look from him to the chief and think: The match is too uneven. But whoever it was would just go on talking in a leisurely way, very respectful toward the chief but also quite unwavering. The chief would issue his ultimatum, and our spokesman would answer that he'd have to report this to the group and bring back word of their decision, because we discussed everything as a group, democratically, but he was pretty sure we would decide as we always had in the past. So the chief would be given more time to think about it. John-i-thin, or whoever it was, would ask some more questions about the ordinance in question, or he would courteously inquire about the population of the town or its economy; and I'd watch the chief's face and it would look hard and proud and bothered, and I'd think: Tonight we'll be in jail. I would wonder how dirty and how cold it was going to be, and how rough they were going to be with us in making the arrests. Then the chief would be saying in a loud voice, "Now look here, if you start running back and forth across the street, disrupting traffic, I'm going to have to call it a parade!" Or he'd be saying, "Now, I'm warning you, if you start sticking your leaflets into parked cars . . ." And I would recognize, sometimes only a moment after he had spoken, that this chief, too, had decided to avoid trouble and was retreating from the stand he had taken, although pretending loudly not to. We always let him pretend.

We talked ourselves in this manner even through towns like Danville, even through Americus—where a few months before they had asked the death penalty for several civil-rights workers, citing an old law against "criminal anarchy." Dave Dellinger, the editor of *Liberation*, came down to walk into Americus with us, and he and

64]

Bradford Lyttle managed those talks, which went on for several days. It was Brad who originated this project (and many others), and he is the Walk's coordinator—very disciplined and cool-headed. Dave is a veteran of many actions, too—with a special gift for making some kind of human contact with the most unlikely people.

None of us slept very well the night before we walked through that town. I remember Yvonne saying with a queer smile, "I think we're going to get clobbered, my friends." The cops in Americus are very free with their night sticks. Police Chief Chambliss had finally declared that (1) we could be sure there would be no trouble and (2) we could be sure that the ordinance against passing out leaflets would be enforced. The two statements contradicted each other. We knew that he knew we were determined to pass out leaflets—both Brad and Dave are unmistakably stubborn, and he wouldn't have misjudged them—so this was either a final warning and he was pretending that he thought we would end by taking it, or it was a way of saving face by refusing to admit in words that he was backing down. Actually what he did was to clear the streets pretty effectively in our path; we passed out leaflets, but we passed out very few. So nobody felt elated by that victory.

This is one reason why, hard as it is, many in the group were almost relieved to have this present battle joined. We had begun to feel that we passed a little too easily through some of these places, our success in doing so meaning too little to those who had actually to live there and struggle for their rights. As transients, ours seemed too special a case. Back in November, when we were jailed in Macon for passing out leaflets, and began to fast, our trial drew a lot of local people, both Negro and white, and some joined a picket line in front of the jail. We began to feel that we were making some kind of a mark.

[65

Then the news of Kennedy's assassination struck: the city decided to get rid of us (our signs about Cuba might cause trouble), so we were released from jail; we halted the Walk for a while; and the battle there was cut short. The jailing at Griffin had been a test, and my friends had met it—at some cost. If their behavior failed to move the Georgia Bureau of Investigation man who tortured them, it moved the sheriff: he acted as go-between for the walkers and city officials, and when my friends held firm in refusing to leave town if released, he obtained for them, within an hour, permission to continue on their way freely. But Albany is a much larger town and a much more complicated situation. If we can make a mark here it will have real meaning.

I have said that we believe in the power of acts to speak louder than words. Even in the negotiations I have described, those officials listened to our words, when they did, because our words enabled them to imagine very clearly what our acts were going to be if they refused us. Then the fact that we spoke with respect for them rather than belligerence allowed them to remain calm enough to weigh what was to their own self-interest in the situation.

Perhaps you will decide, after this description, that even these talks of ours were violent, because they involved a kind of threat. But isn't the decisive question: *what* do we threaten? If we threaten to damage or destroy our antagonists, then, as I see it, we are violent. If we "threaten" a certain kind of trouble for them, or if when they won't listen we proceed to make it, I deny that we do them violence—unless we forget to be careful. Bayard Rustin likes to speak of "creative mischief." I think it is a very good phrase.

Here we are, claiming a basic right, both constitutional and, simply, human: the right to communicate freely with others. And our message seems to us urgent—a message about dangers and about hopes that involve all mankind. (As I tried to plead in the Albany court, it really no longer makes sense for men to use the word "outsiders" about one another: the nuclear age has made us neighbors in a new sense, and we *have* to be able to talk with one another.) But the people of Albany don't want people speaking freely, for a simple reason: they don't want Negroes to be able to speak out. So when we insist, they call us disturbers of their peace. When we disregard the ordinance they have drawn up specially to abridge free speech, they accuse us of defying law and order. Their peace *should* be disturbed; it is a false peace. And the order of which they speak is no true order; there are too many people for whose legitimate desires it allows no room.

Going to jail here has cost us a great deal, but it has also gained us the opportunity to say just this to them more forcibly than we otherwise could have. They would certainly not listen to us if we tried to say it to them in mere words. Nonviolent action is a dramatic technique. Do you remember where in *Hamlet* the prince cries, "The play's the thing"? Hoping to "catch the conscience of the king," he has a drama staged for the king to watch. We go further and try to involve our antagonists as actors in the play, to make it that much more real to them, and hoping to catch if not their consciences—sometimes very elusive—at least that sense in them of what will help or hurt their "image," a practical matter. Or we might possibly catch the consciences of others in the community, without whose acquiescence they cannot behave as they do.

Our hope is to make it hard for them to look away from certain facts. (Gandhi called nonviolence "clinging to the truth.") Like so many others who hold power, they are

[67

adept at dismissing pleas, even at persuading themselves that no real discontent exists; and adept, too, at disposing of those who persist in crying that it does. The play into which we draw them must make it hard for them to do this, and it must at the same time make it possible for them to imagine a new situation fairer to us all.

So we try to assert by our actions a number of different things simultaneously. In the first place, we assert: You cannot easily be rid of us; here we are and we refuse to disappear. They throw us into jail—with the gesture of throwing us away. We serve our sentences and immediately turn up again, to repeat the act for which they arrested us. Ideally our numbers would double every time they tried by *their* actions to say: You are not there. But we haven't done too badly. Fourteen of us tried to walk on December 23. After their trial, six more people, drawn to Albany from various parts of the country by news of our struggle, turned up at the courthouse and stood out in pouring rain to protest the sentences. They were jailed. Three days later, another supporter was walking up and down out there, with a sign about the fast and the special danger Ray Robinson was in because of his water fast. The city decided to terminate all the sentences on the same day, January 15, even for this demonstrator, just arrested—hoping we would go away now and let them forget us. But on January 27, seventeen of us were there again trying to walk the forbidden route. And four days before that, you'll remember, Yvonne Klein and a S.N.C.C. worker, Phil Davis, had been arrested for picketing a civil-defense exercise. On February 3, nine more of us were standing with our signs out at Turner Air Force Base. Two of these people had come all the way from Canada to join us. We have word that there is at least one other supporter in town who may decide to take some action. Now and then one of the cops asks nervously

68]

how many people we plan to bring in. We are not exactly Hydra-headed, but our numbers do increase enough to worry them.

And there is always the possibility that the Negro community will begin to move. The walkers who are outside speak at mass meetings. On New Year's Day a certain number of people in the local movement took part in a sympathy fast. The leaders are wary about moving, still bitterly discouraged by the results of their earlier campaign, which ended in frustration (perhaps because in that particular campaign Martin Luther King did *not* persist); but there is always just the chance that our struggle will give them heart again. Two Negro students joined the six people protesting in the rain on January 8. (I was waiting across the street to observe the arrest, taking shelter in a telephone booth. I ran out of the booth to stare: my friends, I thought, had suddenly learned to sing. The students who had decided to join them, Mamie Ford and Dear Christian, have two of the most beautiful and resonant voices in Albany.) They escaped arrest because Pritchett waited for the rain to stop before he had the group dragged in—the next morning—and they were then in school.

We assert: Here we are and we won't disappear. We assert at the same time, stubbornly: Our wills are our own. Those who hold power here are accustomed, like so many people, to treat others as though they were simply extensions of themselves; they think of "their" Negroes, of their "hands" at the mill—hands, exactly, there simply to carry out their wishes. We keep reminding them of the difference between their wishes and ours; we refuse to let them forget that they are imposing on us.

So when they arrest us, for example, most of us refuse to step meekly into the paddy wagon. It is their will that we go to jail, not ours. We don't try to run away or to

[69

struggle with them; we let them take us; but this is the point: we let *them* do it. (Just as one has a basic right not to testify against oneself in court, we feel we have a right not to put ourselves in jail when arrested unjustly.) Let it be on their shoulders—quite literally. They cannot simply by arresting us dismiss our dissent. Let them feel the weight of it, as they drag or carry us.

And once we are in jail, we say by our fasting: If you want to lead our lives for us, then don't expect us to help. There is a pacifist clergyman, the Reverend Maurice McCrackin, who refuses to pay taxes because they are spent on armaments. When he was arrested back in 1958, he made the government officials carry him. They could not take possession of his conscience, he told them, but "take the body." Another pacifist, Corbett Bishop, arrested for defying the Military Service Act, went so far as to refuse to walk to the bathroom in jail. They finally threw him out of jail as too much of a nuisance. None of us goes as far as Corbett Bishop, but by our fasting we do declare—though this is not all that we declare by it: We refuse to help you take care of us in here.

By our refusal to cooperate, we keep reminding them of our dissent, refusing to allow them the godlike sense that their will alone exists. We make it psychologically more difficult for them to frustrate us. We also make it inconvenient for them, and we make it expensive. It costs the city something to put us up in jail. When we fast, there are also medical expenses. At the end of the first jail-in the Albany *Journal* estimated that we had cost the city five hundred dollars a day. We tax their minds, their muscles, their pocketbooks.

At this point I can suddenly hear you interrupting: "You may be making things difficult for them; I'm sure that you are. But they can make things still more difficult for you, don't forget." You wrote in your letter that

70]

we "ignore like ostriches" the likelihood that by acting as we do we simply increase their anger and impatience. You say they are bound already "by a hundred cords of 'face,' tradition, job," and by our defiance we tighten these bonds—provoking them to be still more harsh with us, really forcing them to be.

If we relied, in our struggle, simply on noncooperation, you would be right, and it *would* be absurd of us to hope to move them. If we asserted by our actions merely that we exist, and our dissent exists, they would be bound to answer simply: Yes, and *we* exist, and it's you or us. Pritchett put it in just these terms as the struggle began: "We'll see who lasts the longest"; and if we saw it in the same terms, we would be wise to give up. Noncooperation, used simply by itself, as a weapon with which to cripple an opponent, can be formidable, of course, as the labor movement discovered; but it could not be formidable in our case. We are so very few. Also, we are strangers, no part of the life of the town. It does not depend in any way either upon our buying power or upon our services. Well, a correction: the men in our group are supposed to go out in work teams, to help sweep the streets and collect the garbage, and they refuse. But this can't be said to disturb the running of the city very seriously. (Eric, we have heard, goes along on the truck for the ride, but does no work—to the amusement of the others on the work gang. They lift him onto the truck as they start out, laughing, and lift him off when they return. One of the men sent us a note about it. Why the guards do nothing I don't know.)

The point is: we don't rely simply on noncooperation, and we don't rely on it as a bludgeon. I have called nonviolent action a dramatic technique, and it is in this context that we resort to it. It is, to be sure, a kind of force; but we are not trying with it to force those opposing us to their knees; we are trying to force them to look at a situation in a new way. (You may call this a nice distinction, and it is, and we have always to keep checking on what we are doing.) We try, I have said, to assert by our actions a number of different things at the same time. This is the key to our hopes. The expression of friendliness can achieve, by itself, surprising effects; it can often stop others from being violent. But one cannot count on this; and anyone would be a fool to count on securing justice by demonstrating friendliness alone. Refusal to cooperate can exert a pressure that has scarcely been appreciated. People are hypnotized by the concept of strength as the ability to take other men's lives. Nevertheless, used as a tactic by itself, especially by a small group—you are right—it is quite as apt to provoke retaliation as it is to gain respect. We count on the special effect that can be achieved when the two pressures—of friendliness and of disobedience—are exerted simultaneously. You have said that we must expect fixed responses from those opposed to us, that a hundred cords bind them tightly, making it impossible for them to behave in any other way than the way in which they do. The effect for which we hope is one precisely of loosening these cords; we hope to shake their minds free of them.

We assert on the one hand: We differ with you, and here we are. They are bound to assert: Here *we* are, you won't do away with us. But we anticipate them and assert at the same time: We do not threaten your person. I think it is St. Augustine who says that to love your neighbor means to let him feel: I wish you to be. We try to assert this—in spite of our disagreement with them. And so we disturb their peace of mind, disturb that "order" in which their minds are used to seeing things. People who defy them are usually unfriendly. The question forces itself upon them: if we do not object to them

72]

personally, why do we object so stubbornly to what they do? They have to examine the issues. At any rate, they are free to; they are not just caught up automatically in the reflex of self-defense. They are used to thinking of their own dignity as inseparable from the respect due the role they play, but by acting with respect toward them as persons and refusing to respect this role, we make it easier for them to draw the distinction too, and to consider taking some unaccustomed action.

We have to be careful to keep a kind of balance between the two pressures we exert upon them. The more uncooperative we are, the more care we have to take to communicate friendliness too. It is hard. The people who refuse to walk, for example, and are dragged upstairs and down, sometimes feel just too physically battered to speak at the moment when there is a chance. Each person has to gauge his own strength in this respect. And we have always to be weighing the question: Would this just provoke them, without making our point? against the question: Are we being too careful of ourselves and making our dissent less real to them than we could? We cannot ever be sure of striking just the right balance. The fact that we cannot, it's clear, bothers you, and you feel that we should always lean over backward to avoid provoking them. It is violence of a sort, you would say, to bring out the worst in another person. I would have to agree with you—if, that is, we fail then, by our response, to reveal that person to himself in a new way. But I would have to add that this is a risk it is not humanly possible to avoid—if we choose to act at all. Even Socrates, Jesus, Gandhi did not avoid bringing out the worst in certain men, whom they provoked to kill them.

And when you give us the counsels that you do, you forget one thing—the violence that exists before we act. It is not that the "worst" is brought out in the segregationist only when peace and freedom walkers pass through. The Negro feels the brunt of it year after year —every time he attempts to act like a free man, and of course every time he fears to. Violence is already active here; it is built into the very structure of the existing society. If we seek a world in which men do the least possible violence to each other (which is to state just the negative of it), then we are committed not simply to try to avoid violence ourselves, but to try to destroy patterns of violence which already exist. We can sometimes hope, by the way, that even if a person provoked to violence against us remains himself unchanged by our response, others witnessing the incident or hearing about it will be changed and will recognize something about the society of which they are a part.

One question that was often discussed among us while the Walk was on the road was whether or not we should be prudent in the South about the way we sat next to one another in the Walk cars—the sight of a white woman sitting next to a Negro man being especially provocative. Agreement was never reached, and I think there was no right or wrong answer to the question. Most people chose to ignore prudence. I have known this choice to be almost disastrous. One day when the walkers had gone through too much already (it was the day they were tortured in Griffin), they had barely the strength left to cope with a situation that flared up in a town just south of Griffin, when a car in which Michele Gloor and Ron Moose were sitting next to each other was stopped by the town's sheriff and surrounded by a group of toughs whom he called over. This day Michele finally changed her place. I have also seen the same choice work very positive re-sults. The sheriff of a county near Americus, a very diffi-cult man who had been harassing us all one day, turned purple with rage at the sight of Erica Enzer sitting in a car next to Ray Robinson. Dave Dellinger happened to be talking with the sheriff at that moment, and when the man, trembling, demanded to know whether we believed in this kind of thing, Dave answered with such calm good nature that we didn't think anything about it that his rage dissolved in astonishment. I was astonished myself at the impression the moment seemed to leave with him.

One thing that inclined most of us to make the more daring choice when we felt at all ready for what might come (we could never be sure we were ready) was Ray's attitude. It disturbed him that the question was even discussed. Didn't we carry a sign calling for "freedom now?" He wondered who was going to listen to us if we didn't even feel free, ourselves, to behave naturally with one another. Ray is a former prize fighter who says he once hated white men so much that he decided to take up boxing so that the world could watch him beat them up. Then "come a new thing to me that's called nonviolence and I'm trying it." But when he joined the Walk in Philadelphia it was hard for him to feel much faith in those of us who were white. As we have lived through all these days together, he has come more and more to believe in the possibility of living at peace with white people, but he is easily shaken in that belief. Every time we dare to act out, ourselves, the way of life we call for, it makes it easier for him to believe. And for others too, of course. Every time we hesitate, we do him and them violence in spite of ourselves. So we have to weigh this, too. In every particular situation, I think, one has to weigh anew what would be violent and what would be nonviolent behavior, and the answer is seldom simple.

Our action in fasting, here in jail, cannot help but be in part provocative—it is so *very* uncooperative. And it makes it difficult for the authorities to know just how to behave. (This is especially so for the city doctor, and our

[75

fasting has certainly brought out the worst in *him;* he is still so confused and angry that he can hardly bring himself to check on how we are.) But we count on the fact that fasting declares finally a great deal more than defiance, and declares it more clearly than any words could. It communicates how serious we are—gives assurance that we are at least convinced in our own minds that our cause is just, or we would hardly subject ourselves to this and persist in it day after day. It communicates too that we want no victory in the usual sense—are not concerned to see how much punishment we can deal out. We are willing to take on ourselves the brunt of suffering. Having declared this, even without words, it is more possible for us to make the further point: we want justice, but if justice means anything, it means that those who have been opposing us will have rights too. It needn't mean defeat in any real sense for anybody.

I have been lying here thinking of an action we might take if we never do succeed in winning our rights in Albany. We might well walk out of the city along the route Pritchett has dictated, handing out a new leaflet which would say: We have lost and accept the fact—we have not enough strength to persist any longer, and we have not enough time (we are supposed to be walking to Cuba); but we hope that as you look back now on what has happened, you will come to consider that our defeat was just as much your defeat. And then the leaflet could elaborate on the importance—to everybody—of breaking down barriers to communication. The truth with which above all we hope to confront the people of Albany, dramatically, is just this: that we need not be antagonists.

There are always what might be called negative advantages to be gained by observing the discipline of nonviolence. Refusal to hit back at an opponent or lie to him or trick him can inhibit him in his resort to violence, break the familiar circuit of vengeance and countervenge-ance. Used as a prudent tactic it is effective. But when those adopting this discipline actually feel a human bond —however frail—with those opposing them and feel a re-sponsibility toward them, and this shapes their vision of a resolution to the struggle, they tap a further source of energy and they can exert still greater pressure. The vision they hold can be to some extent hypnotic. (This, by the way, is a reason why going to jail holds a particular meaning for many of us. Here our sense of being related to all men is greatly sharpened, for we cross a distance that once seemed awesome and separated us from all those whom society has cast out.)

It is the genius of the song that is the freedom move-ment's hymn that it sounds all the notes I have been talk-ing about—stubborn on the one hand, reassuring on the other. The words go, "We shall overcome . . . We are not afraid"; and in the same breath, "Black and white to-gether, we shall live in peace someday." You may remind me that most white people are deaf to the song. You may remind me, too, that the majority of Negroes in the move-ment profess to believe in nonviolence only as a tactic. Nevertheless, those in the revolt with a vision of "the be-loved community" have put a stamp on the movement— as the song reveals. As for the deafness of most white people, the song is realistic here; it goes, "We shall over-come *some day*," and the music gives these last two words a strong accent.

One thing that makes nonviolent struggle difficult is that usually one must wait so long to see the effects of one's actions. The effect of a violent act is immediately visible. One who relies on violence hopes to solve a prob-lem by cutting others off from him. The break can be made quickly enough. (This is exactly how I would define a violent act, by the way: it is one that denies another

[77

person's existence or the existence of his dissenting will; a wholly violent act literally cuts off his life.) One who relies on nonviolence hopes to force the other person to acknowledge a human relationship and to act accordingly.

What we must hope is that those who oppose us, and whom we have provoked not to reflex action but to reflection, will begin to weigh, in spite of themselves, the complex truth we have dramatized. Given the fact that we care as stubbornly as we do for what we assert to be our rights; given the fact that it is inconvenient and expensive to deny us; given the fact that we refuse to treat our opponents as enemies, do not wish to humiliate them, but are willing to suffer ourselves for what we ask—they must weigh whether or not they are willing to deny the human bond between us, which we assert; whether they are willing not so much to *take* any more punishment, which is the question raised by violent struggle, but to deal out any more punishment, or at least to be seen to be willing.

We can be grateful that they must take into account the opinions of other people not only in their own community but outside it. They hate to have to. I have heard the secretary of the Albany Movement, Marion Page, exclaim, "They would like, in spite of the words of Donne, to think Albany an island, entire unto itself." But they cannot, quite. Too many business ties now link Albany with "the main." So we can hope still that our actions will move this group or that group of people—who knows from which direction—to speak out in our behalf, or to speak behind the scenes.

One thing we never feel sure about, of course, is how many people will learn of our action. We send out our press releases; those of us outside jail often sit up all night stuffing envelopes; but whether or not any of the major newspapers or magazines decides to cover the story seems sometimes almost a matter of whim. To date we have had most coverage in the home towns of some of the walkers —Denver, Minneapolis, Albuquerque. The New York *Times,* someone tells us, dislikes fasts. If one of us should die, I suppose . . . At any rate, we live in an age in which a story *can,* if it is picked up, be spread in a matter of hours around the world.

One has time in here to dream, and I dream sometimes that this and other new facts about the present age will make it the age in which people finally decide that nonviolent struggle is the only kind of struggle from which they can hope much. It is of course the age in which we are for the first time able to destroy ourselves entirely if we fail to decide this. "We must abolish the weapons of war before they abolish us," Kennedy acknowledged—though he failed to match the words with any very bold action. Auden has written, "We must love one another or die." It is for the first time in history necessary for us to learn to struggle with one another not as enemies but as members of one human family. It is also perhaps for the first time really possible. Modern communications, as well as all the complex ties that have been established by their means, make us now more effectively that one family. In earlier ages people could tyrannize over one another in convenient isolation; world opinion did not exist as an inhibiting force to be invoked. But now what men in other parts of the world think is a matter of practical concern. And in another sense too it is more realistic than in other ages to appeal to men's consciences—or to their wish to appear to behave with conscience: one could say that it is for the first time in history really feasible to establish just societies, in which men act toward other men—everywhere—with that sense of responsibility which members of the same family show. It is the age of abundance, and it can no longer be argued that some people have to be exploited so that others may live decently. If something is necessary, and also feasible, one can dream that it will happen. Necessity is at least sometimes the mother of invention. One verse of the freedom movement's hymn begins, "The truth shall make us free." Who knows whether or not men will recognize the truth in time?

And who knows whether or not we will succeed in communicating the truth we are attempting to act out here in Albany? At least we can still hope to.

SIX

Yvonne gets up from the lower bunk where she has been lying and looks on the steel ledge of the door for her paper cup, to get herself a drink. Hers is the blood-stained cup—she has marked it VAMPIRA; her gums have been bleeding more and more. From a top bunk, Edie asks, "Who has the tape measure?" There is a daily ritual now of taking our diminishing measurements, and as they are read out we pretend to be delighted. "Everyone think thin!" Edie has written in one of the notes we have sent the men in our group. The thinner we get, the more the authorities will have to worry. The more we'll have to worry, too, of course, but there is a conspiracy among us to forget dread and see in our fading only the occasion for congratulations. "Edie, wow, chick!" Ray has written in a note after seeing us at the trial. "You look like one of these women one see in the movies, with a tight tight girdle, so tight that it looks as though you tried to make it touch, side to side. . . . Candy, you look great, like a little wax doll. . . . Yvonne, wow, your husband won't know you!" Yvonne was overweight when the fast began; now she is quite svelte, but, large-boned, broad-shoul-dered, she gives an impression still of unusual strength. Watching her, I remember how often on the Walk I have drawn calm from the sight of her, moving along the road with her particular stubborn pace that kept up easily with the others yet managed to seem almost languorous—as the pace of cattle will, moving quite quickly across a field—

her shoulders sloped forward slightly, her feet never lifted very high. She stands with the cup in her hand. I see her legs begin to waver under her with the peculiar undulating motion I have seen once before, her knees rubber. She is falling.

I am the nearest to her and jump up from my bunk as quickly as I can and throw my arm out around her, going down too, to try to keep her from crashing against the pipes of the sink; but I am not quick enough to prevent it entirely. She slumps there on the floor for a moment, her slack weight against me, and her eyes stare ahead of her without focus. Slowly they uncloud; she struggles up, not wanting help. "I'm all right."

She rests for a moment, leaning against one of the bunks. Someone recovers her cup for her and she takes a drink. Then she climbs up to the bunk where Edie sits, reaches for the pack of cards we have, and the two of them begin a game of gin rummy. I lie down again, shaken. Slow-motion, in my head—and against my body —she falls again. I think: The endurance test really begins. I have watched with unbelief as, day after day, my companions have held up without food—Edie exclaiming in mock lament, "I seem to grow stronger and stronger!" though she thins down like a sucked peppermint stick. I had begun to feel a little like a mortal among immortals. Could they somehow in Hamlet's wild words "eat the air, promise-crammed"? But they are mortal too; they can fall. I think suddenly of how easily Yvonne, just now, could have cracked her head open against the sink; feel again, with new force, how real are the risks we take in here. We are putting from us, intentionally, one kind of power, on which most people rely. I feel again the reality of this, feel again our frailty.

The cards go slap, slap, slap, briskly; and in the distant cell block where some of our men are held I hear the wavering strains of Peter Gregonis' harmonica. He is blowing a shaky version of *Freedom Boat*. A verse of the song shapes itself in my head:

> *Jordan's waters are chilly and cold,*
> *Hallelujah!*
> *Chill the body but not the soul!*
> *Hallelujah!*

Hope flares up in me again. Yes, hallelujah! Then a question just hovers: *not* the soul?

A hubbub starts in the other part of the jail. Cries. Countercries. A scuffle. Laughter. We hear a cop going in there: "Hey! The cells aren't to play in!"

MONDAY, FEBRUARY 10 (15TH DAY)

At eight-thirty I have awakened to eat part of the breakfast shoved into the cell to me along the floor on a tin plate. Grits. A few sips of coffee, for the sugar in it and the warmth. The yolk of the fried egg. I have left the white of the egg and the bread and the sausage—still wanting to be part of the fast in token. I have slid the plate back into the corridor and then turned over to sleep some more—and have dreamed:

A huge old-fashioned wood-burning stove stands in the room, scalding hot. I notice suddenly that Edic has her hand lying on its top, and she doesn't seem to realize that she has it there; it is beginning to smoke. I snatch it off. Then I see that another of my companions—is it Michele or is it Yvonne?—is curled on the top of the stove, napping. She too begins to burn. I try to lift her off, but she is terribly heavy and I try to speak to her, but her eyes are clouded and I cannot waken her. I feel a deathly clumsiness.

[83

I waken with a start. Dr. Hilsman has come into the cell to give vitamin shots. With him are Pritchett's pretty blond secretary and one of the cops, Sergeant Hamilton. My friends don't cooperate on these visits, as they consider the vitamins nourishment, so each time the doctor's assistants, tugging and pulling, have to turn the patients over for him. Yvonne is getting the first injection this morning. She is lying drugged with sleep, though her eyes are open. As they turn her over, a lock of her hair is shaken loose, and it lies across her mouth; she is unaware of it. I stare at her. Her lips are slightly parted in a smile, and the smile seems to me sharply familiar. I have sat by my aunt's deathbed as, half waking again and again from a coma, she has gazed in front of her, studying the face of her approaching death, with just such a smile on her lips.

I try to shake off this memory and also the memory of my dream. The doctor gives Edie an injection next. Erica's turn will be tomorrow. As he hands me a vitamin pill, I mention to him that Yvonne has fainted, and he stands there for a moment, then grunts. He announces, "She'd better start eating," and he leaves us.

Clarence, the prison run-around, appears at the bars, sleepy-faced, and thrusts in to us a note on toilet paper. It is from Tony Brown:

"Dear Personable Pacifists of Prodigious Patience and Persuasion—did I ever tell you you're

All beautiful
and courageous
and joyous
and delightful
and uplifting
and missed
and loved by us all?"

He confides: "My taste at this time is toward creamed

dishes—mushroom soup, creamed carrots, creamed peas, creamed cauliflower with cheese sauce . . ."

An arm comes around from the next-door cell, Michele's, handing us a joint note to the men that they have begun in there. Michele's note ends:

"Friends, here is a serious matter. Would ice cream be as good hot as cold? How does hot spumoni ice cream sound to you? I'm tired of thinking of soups . . ."

Edie begins her letter:

"Hello, fabulous fasters of filosophical felicity . . . I am getting very turned on to marshmallow sauce on fruit salad and also omelet filled with either strawberry or cherry preserves . . ."

And Yvonne writes:

". . . Hilsman has told me that I ought to eat. And I will, too, and you know when. And what." (She has sent them her suggested menus before this.) "I love you all."

Now it is later, almost noon, and we are waiting for a visit from A. J. Muste. Pritchett has read us a telegram announcing his arrival. Dave Dellinger may be coming too. "Oh magic!" Michele has written to the men. Their arrival has proved magic of a kind on this Walk before. Dave helped to negotiate our way through Americus, A. J. to negotiate our way through Atlanta, the second time we walked in that city, when we returned there from Macon after Kennedy's assassination and held a walk of mourning, on Thanksgiving Day. The police first gave permission, then abruptly canceled it—storming all of a sudden into the house where we were staying and threatening to arrest us as vagrants. A. J. devised a timing and a route for us that probably changed their minds again: with Martin Luther King's permission, we made our start at the church where King was delivering a sermon that morning, and the authorities must have considered

[85

the nature of the publicity that might result from an arrest. No arrest was made. We are wondering what new thoughts may occur to A. J. about our situation here.

Twelve o'clock. We hear the bell of the clock on the tower of the county sheriff's office across the street "bonging" the hour, as Ray has decribed it—"Dig that word 'bonging.'" Footsteps. It is A. J., escorted by Sergeant Bass, who is telling him roughly that he's not to stay too long and he's not to hand us any papers. As quickly as we can we climb up onto the top bunks, to make it easier for him to talk with us. He stands there in the narrow corridor, a little flustered by the cop's rudeness, peering into our two cells. Next to the bullying cop, how skinny and gray he looks; he looks his almost eighty years, looks made of paper. The sergeant strolls away. Edie, who has worked for A. J. before joining the Walk, presses forward, and he draws nearer, too, and by thrusting their faces between the bars, they manage to kiss. He studies us. His long knobby-knuckled hands, moving against the bars as though to remove them, as though to touch us, are trembling. His voice trembles a little, too. I remember suddenly how it used to feel to visit the prisoners in these cages while Pritchett still allowed me; I remember the remark of a friend the first time I went off to jail: "You don't know what it's like to be locked *out*."

He makes his report to us. He has already seen Pritchett and the city manager, Stephen Roos; and he has found the Chief very rigid, Roos perhaps a little less so. Pritchett made angry reference to a talk Brad Lyttle gave at a mass meeting before the second jailing—in which he urged the Albany Movement to consider group fasting as a good way to make a battle too expensive for the city. Pritchett always has his spies at these meetings, he let A. J. know. Then he referred stiffly to a remark Kit made to a Denver newspaperman during a quick visit home. It was relayed by the press, and Pritchett read it in an Atlanta paper: "If we can only break Pritchett on this one issue . . ." A. J. comments, "This was the wrong way of putting it, of course—as we are *not* out to break any *person*." Kit speaks from the next cell, distressed. She has already seen the quotation in the Atlanta paper and been disturbed about it, and she explains again that the remark has been plucked out of context; the interview she had given was in quite another spirit. A. J. nods, an anxious figure still. On the top of his lean head a tuft of fine white hair stands up, like the crest of a bird, blowing slightly in the air. Behind his glasses, his eyes, which can sometimes light up like a fire, are dull. He tries now to strike a more hopeful note. He repeats that Roos seems a little less rigid than Pritchett and even mentioned vaguely the possibility that the ordinance under which we were arrested might someday be abolished. And they have both, at least, left the door open for further talks.

After he has gone I lie thinking: we have certainly made mistakes. As I wrote to my friend, a very necessary statement to make to antagonists in a struggle like this is that we are not out to work them harm. Here in the paranoid South it is especially necessary. How complicated it can be to keep this in mind! Brad had chosen for very logical reasons to stress at the mass meeting how costly to the city one could make a nonviolent challenge. The badly discouraged Albany Movement needed to hear this. But Pritchett, listening in, needed to hear again that we were not really out for blood. Poor Kit never dreamed that her remark would reach Pritchett's ears. Perhaps one had always to assume that one spoke in his hearing.

And of course we had also made our mistakes where we could not plead the excuse of speaking for certain ears only. I remember the first day of our trials after our second jail-in. A few among us laughed out loud at the

[87

tactics of the city attorney, Grady Rawls, as he tried to imply that we were all obviously Communists. There had been laughter, too, simply at his grotesque personal behavior. For while the defense had the floor he sat with his feet up on a table, his great bulk sagged in his chair at disdainful ease. Once he didn't even bother to rise when his turn came to speak. Our laughter had been conspicuous enough to cause him to burst out, "These people have no respect for anything!" Throughout the course of the Walk, I recall, one of the mistakes hardest for us to avoid has always been the mistake of laughing at our opponents. There is such relief in it for us.

But how grave have our mistakes been? Naturally Pritchett would bring up what grievances he could, in resisting accommodation with us. But isn't there evidence that he and others too recognize that we do *not* stand in the usual relation of adversaries? When I made my statement in court I pleaded that we had been moved to act as we had, not by a feeling of contempt for the people of Albany, as Attorney Rawls charged, but by a feeling of kinship; that what brought us here was a desire to talk with them, at the very deepest level possible; that it troubled us to be called outsiders, because we felt that a time in history had arrived when men could no longer afford to think of other men as outsiders. We were too bound to one another now; the actions of a group of people anywhere in the world could drastically affect the lives of other people anywhere else in the world, so how could one speak of outsiders any longer in the old sense? As I developed this theme I was surprised to find with what real attention Pritchett, Judge Durden, even Attorney Rawls listened. They gave me their attention, I decided later, partly because I was so exhausted that day that it took a certain deliberate physical effort on my part to get my words out—and they were hypnotized by this.

88]

But it was not only that. Hadn't my words matched something they really couldn't help observing in our attitude from the beginning?

I remind myself of the occasional startling responses of some of the cops. I think of the day Sergeant Cress heard a radio somewhere in the jail and suspected that we had it. We denied it, but he asked us to step out of the cell so that he could search. Most of us were committed not to walk while in jail, and we reminded him that he would have to carry us out if he really couldn't trust us to be speaking the truth. He stepped angrily in among us, at that, and grabbed Candy under the arms and jerked her out into the corridor. In doing so, he accidentally dragged her against Michele, knocking Michele's head hard against the bars; she burst into tears. Pritchett came along just then and decided to take our word about the radio, and Cress vanished, but he reappeared immediately after Pritchett had gone. Kneeling down, he asked to see the bump on Michele's head and put his hand out clumsily through the bars to touch it, telling her, "I didn't mean to hurt you, you know. Are we still friends?"

I remember Assistant Chief Moore on a later day. Candy's mother had made a trip south to visit her. On the day of her arrival she was permitted to come back to her cell, but the next day Moore, in charge, suddenly decided to rule that Candy could only see her if she would break her commitment not to walk, and walk out to the front office and back. When she held to her word, he worked on her feelings without mercy, chiding her. "Well, you certainly broke her up! If you could see her crying out there!" Candy was reduced to tears herself, though she still refused to be bullied. Later, as some of us were writing notes to Candy's mother, Moore reappeared, to ask "Do you like me any better now, Candy?" To our amazement, his question seemed to be without sarcasm.

[89

I assure myself that clearly both of these cops recognize that we offer a kind of friendship even as we struggle with them and clearly too, unlikely as it might seem, they put some sort of value upon it.

I think of a gesture Pritchett himself made on the day Ray returned from the psychiatric ward, where the Chief had managed to break his will to water-fast. Ray had some writings he had been wanting me to see, and on the very day the Chief boasted to us that he had outwitted Ray, he appeared at our cell with the writings in his hand, in the unlikely role of Ray's messenger. "Another first!" Edie wrote to the men. "Head Camper just turned into run-around!"

But how much can I read into these incidents? How much hope for us do they hold? Can I say to myself: They are still fighting us, without any scruples, but we are winning their friendship? Or must I say: We are winning their friendship, but they are still fighting us, and without any scruples?

I think again of how much easier it is to measure the effects of violent struggle. And I remember suddenly a passage in George Orwell's *Homage to Catalonia* that has always haunted me: the author, visiting the Loyalist lines during the Spanish civil war, lies out on a hillside watching as Franco artillery tries to place a hit on a certain Loyalist installation, and after a while he finds himself, in spite of himself, as the enemy fire goes wide of the mark, wanting them to make the hit—wanting it just out of a certain perverse spirit of neatness. Yes, even against all reason, something in us likes to be able to count off: this has been hit now, and this, and this, and this. In the struggle in which we are engaged, we can make no count of our own hits. Guesses will have to do us. Our evidence can only be "the evidence of things not seen . . . things hoped for." Yes, hope will have to satisfy us.

A man in a distant cell is calling to his wife in a cell nearer to us:

"Vickie!"

"What?" Her reply is mumbled, utterly weary.

"Vickie!"

She speaks a little louder: "What?"

"What did he say? What did he tell you?"

"Nothing."

"What are we going to do?"

Silence. Then she raises her voice: "You certainly fixed me."

He is quiet for a few moments. Then: "Do you love me?"

Very flatly, more to herself than to him: "No. I'm gonna leave you."

He calls, "Don't say that, Vickie!"

She doesn't answer.

He calls, "Vickie! Vickie!"

Not even bothering to raise her voice now so that he can hear her, she states, "You'll never change."

Now it is four-thirty. A guard shoves into the cell for me the second of the two meals for the day. I reach under the bunk for a magazine to put the greasy plate on. Then I bend my spine into a curve so that I can sit up without my head knocking the upper bunk. I tuck my feet under my skirt and lean back against the wall, trying to be as little visible as possible while I eat. Yvonne has returned to her bunk across the way and is resting there. As I pick up the small red plastic fork which has been dumped into the middle of the food—and first lick the handle clean and then lick my fingers clean (there is no napkin ever)—I look across at her, and she is watching me, in spite of herself, fascinated. The bologna I leave. It's not hard to resist it. There are also diced turnips today, grits, black-eyed peas. To eat in here always seems to me a gross act—not only because my friends are fasting, but because I feel like a caged animal being fed. The food itself is gross. The grits are easiest to get down. The turnips have a bitter, slightly dirty taste, but I get them down too. I put a forkful of black-eyed peas in my mouth. And then my stomach abruptly revolts. The peas are very thick and pasty and, like the turnips, somehow dirty in taste. They are very nearly daily fare, and I realize with alarm that I just cannot force them down my throat any more. I have pulled myself out of the trouble I was in by beginning to eat a little more now each day—to eat a part of breakfast —and I ask myself: What will happen if my stomach begins to refuse what is put before me? Fear for myself flares up in me for a moment, and then I manage to quiet it. I slide the plate out into the corridor and around the corner a little so my friends won't have to look at it. I get up to wash my sticky hands; I lie down again and try to rest. George is calling to Vickie again:

"Vickie! Vickie!"

Finally: "What?"

"They haven't let me make a phone call yet."

A weary grunt.

"Vickie! Do you love me?"

Again: "No. I'm gonna leave you."

"Vickie!"

No answer.

"If you don't love me, why did you call me 'alligator' then? Vickie!"

No answer.

"Victoria!"

The speaking of her full name draws an answer: "What?"

"You gonna leave me?"

"Yes. You certainly fixed me."

He is quiet for a while. Then: "Forgive me? Oblata?"
She doesn't answer.

A long silence. Then he calls again, in a voice small and sweet and cunning: "I'll miss your stuffed cabbage!"

When Sergeant Bass told A. J. that his time was up, we asked him if he would open one of the windows on our corridor for a little while. The air of the prison seems particularly rank and stifling today. Our request is usually ignored, and Bass didn't even reply, but now he returns and props open the window across from Kit and Michele and Mary and Candy. A draft of air from the alley pierces the prison air and we gasp, taken by surprise in spite of ourselves; there is so sharp a difference. For a while nobody speaks. We draw it into our lungs; the simple untainted air is as distinct to our palates as wine. I lie tasting it, an agreeable lightness spreading through my limbs.

Suddenly we hear our names called from the alley. Everybody who isn't on a top bunk climbs up to be able to see. Erica stands on the crossbars of the door, as though it were a ladder. She has managed to wash her hair today in the small sink, and, still damp, it stands out from her head in a bush. There in the alley is Carl Arnold—the young Negro poet who joined us in Atlanta and went to jail our first time in here but is helping outside this time —and next to him is Peter Light, a Canadian student who came down a few days after Mary Suzuki and Michael Newman. Mary has told us that he is planning to get himself arrested soon. They are both smiling up at us, Peter a little anxious—pale and tall and skinny, with a long neck, with a large thin beak of a nose; Carl shy, graceful, and very much more debonair.

Why are there no cops around to seize them? Mary is concerned for Peter. He is calling to her that someday soon he may try to pass out leaflets in front of City Hall.

[93

She calls a warning: "Peter, be careful! You may be coming in *today!*" He cannot quite hear her. "What, Mary?"

Carl calls something now which *we* cannot hear, so he calls next, "Do you want to see us or hear us?" If they step nearer the building, we will be able to hear them better, but they will be out of our sight. "Both! Both!" we cry.

Mary calls to Peter, "My pulse is eighty today!" He still cannot hear. "What? What?" Somebody warns, "He may think you're saying that you ate today!" She shouts, "I'm writing you a note!" Peter shouts, trying to make these words very distinct, "They are holding sympathy demonstrations in Canada!" We shout, "Hurrah!"

Every now and then they both turn their heads quickly from side to side, to see if anyone is coming. Carl calls, "Do you need anything?" Edie calls, "Crayons!" Mary calls to Peter, "I'll try to throw a note to you out the window!"

She rolls the note she has written into a little ball; we see her arm reach out and toss it. It misses. The window doesn't open up and down but is tilted in, and so the toss has to be just right. Kit takes off her belt and fishes the note back from the corridor where it has dropped. Mary tosses it a second time, and again it misses, and again Kit fishes it back. "Wait!" Peter calls. And now his voice is close to the window. He has found something to stand on; suddenly we see his hand appear. Mary reaches out again—strains—reaches. We hold our breath. The two hands just touch. Peter takes the note.

As their hands touch, we all begin to bounce up and down on our knees on the bunks. We look at each other and laugh. Outside, Carl and Peter jump into the air, laughing too. Carl unslings a camera from his shoulder and aims it up at us. Erica, remembering her wild hair, exclaims, "You mustn't take my picture this way!" Everybody laughs at that. Then suddenly the two men look quickly to one side, raise their hands to us and vanish. They must have seen the "fuzz." We wait a little, listening for sounds of their being dragged in, but there is no such commotion. They are safe.

We cannot stop smiling at each other—as though their visit has been of some extraordinary significance. I feel, in fact, quite as though the bars of the jail have suddenly given way for us; the city of Albany has tried to put us away, but it can't; we can't be isolated, can't be held. A verse from one of the freedom songs bursts out in my head:

> *The only chain that a man can stand*
> *Is the chain of hand in hand!*

We'll join hands finally even with them.

I am quite aware that my sudden optimism is irrational. The fact that Peter and Mary have managed to touch hands through the window has, obviously enough, no relevance to our situation. But it is like a sign that speaks to us. In this struggle we are unable to measure our hopes literally. So to keep our hope alive we feed on symbols. I remember one morning waking to see a small sparrow, perched on a rusty pipe against the brick wall facing us outside, fluffing its feathers in a patch of sunlight; and I remember how hungrily I concentrated all my attention upon it—feeling: yes, there is hope for us, yes, there is hope.

I hear Vickie calling to George: "Hey, knucklehead! Are you still worrying about me?"

He calls eagerly, "Yes. Are you about me?"

There is a long silence. Then she calls, "I forgive you this time."

[95

He calls, "Do you love me?"

She calls back, "If I didn't love you, why would I stick by you?" And she begins to laugh, and he begins to laugh, too.

"Okay," he calls, "okay!"

SEVEN

I<small>T IS</small> a little later. Footsteps. A brisk knock on the wall beyond our cells. "C. B.!" everyone cries, sitting up.

It is C. B. King on his daily visit to bring us our mail. Sometimes his associate, Attorney Thomas Jackson, is with him too—tall and shy, a little smile twisting the neat line of his narrow mustache. Today he is by himself. "And how are the ladies today?" He opens his briefcase and begins to sort the bundles of letters. Some are for us, some for the men in the cell block around the corner, some for the men in the "hole," some for Bradford in the county jail across the street.

Edie reaches out her hands: "Oh hurry, C. B.!"

He tells her, "I expect from all of you a saintly patience." He looks at me. "How is Miss Deming today?"

He teases me with the formal address, though he calls the others by their first names. I tell him that I am really out of trouble now, but that Yvonne fainted yesterday. A shadow passes across his face. Then he begins to hand out the mail.

The time of this daily visit, too, is a time when the bars of our cell seem for a moment to melt. It is not only that he brings us letters and takes ours safely out. As Yvonne and Edie begin to banter with him now—"You're wearing a beautiful sweater today, C. B." (it is a soft lavender), "My sweater meets with your approval?" (deadpan)—I think of the distance we have traveled toward each other.

When the Walk entered Albany, a good many of us

had entertained naïve hopes about the welcome we would receive from people in the Albany Movement. We took it for granted that if we engaged in a struggle with the authorities here, Movement people would welcome the opportunity to renew their own battle in coordination with ours. Instead we found them wary of making any move at all. We were invited to a number of their leadership meetings, and at these meetings one man, Reverend Samuel Wells, kept suggesting demonstrations in our support—"If people are fasting, we should be moving quickly; that's not a play toy." (He has fasted himself in jail here.) But the Movement's president, Slater King (C. B.'s brother), and its secretary, Marion Page, and C. B. himself had always urged that they think about it a while longer. "We need more than faith," C. B. had commented to Wells.

We might, really, have anticipated this caution, because we had first met most of these people—a few weeks before, in Macon—when we attended some sessions of the trials which the federal government was conducting against them. They had submitted to Washington any number of complaints about abuses they had suffered from the Albany authorities, and no action had been taken; but when a local white merchant filed a complaint against *them*, in connection with the boycott they had started, the federal government had decided to prosecute —"a bone thrown to the segregationists," as one civil-rights lawyer put it. It was little wonder that their present mood was one of discouragement.

But it wasn't only that they were discouraged. They were obviously skeptical about us, too. We learned with shock that some of them even believed the rumor the white community had spread that we were Communists. C. B. never took that rumor seriously, but his attitude toward us was one of great reserve.

98]

I remember a long talk I had with him back in December, the day before our group first walked into Albany. I didn't walk with them that day, because I was called to appear in court in Macon—having volunteered to appeal the constitutionality of our earlier arrest there. C. B. was my lawyer and drove me up. Ron Moose came along as a witness. As we drove through the sad countryside, past the unpainted shacks with collapsing porches where Negroes lived—hard to decide, often, which shacks were abandoned and which still lived in—I remember talking eagerly about my hopes that the struggle for civil rights and the struggle for disarmament would become one. C. B. listened courteously. On the subject of disarmament he posed the usual questions about whether one could abandon all national defense, then listened quietly as I argued the necessity of adopting nonviolent defense now that we lived in the nuclear age. Yes, he could see that men should take this new step; but would they? And then he confided that he had not, for himself, given the subject much thought. When you were a Negro —when you were down in a ditch and the white man had his foot on your throat—you didn't often look beyond the ditch and the struggle there.

I was to see him that day in the Macon courtroom and later in the courtroom at Albany, waging his own hard combat, which is brilliant, impeccable, and again and again frustrated. Albany: the cops slouch in their chairs, their caps set on their heads askew as they joke with one another; the prosecutor, in his loose suit rumpled as an elephant's skin, dreams with his feet up, enjoying his cigar. C. B. enters. His face is alert and his back straight; the crease in his trousers is a careful one. As the arguments begin, his words, too, are careful, and they are full of style, in contrast to the drawled and grunted statements of most of those who speak for the prosecution.

[99

Out of language he has made for himself a precise sword and a polished shield, and he moves in close to his opponents; he plays a daring game—again and again moves up to the very boundary of open contempt for them. The argument he presents is always clear and carefully reasoned; everyone in the court can follow it; but he delights, too, in using certain words here and there with which his opponents are probably unfamiliar—as he delights in repeating, deadpan, with a question mark attached, a word one of them has misused or a phrase that is ungrammatical. They pretend, all of them, that none of this is happening—pretend that this is just old C. B., Albany nigger, doing a little ungainly dance and shuffle for them. They yawn and turn away.

"Now, C. B.," drawls the Chief.

"Yes, Laurie," says C. B. quietly.

The judge raps sharply with his gavel, and the Chief turns to him: "I don't want him to address me by that name."

C. B.: "I am no more appreciative of his addressing me as C. B."

The judge: "We're going to proceed in an orderly manner. His official title is Chief Pritchett."

C.B.: "I say respectfully that my official title is Attorney King."

The judge: "We're going to proceed."

Whether C. B. is arguing for one of us or for some local Negro client, the ruling is against him, invariably. He has not been known to win one case in this courtroom. But week after week he reappears, a bitter but persistent figure; outmatches them all again, and again is judged the loser.

I remember the trip up to Macon with him, and I remember the trip back. At my trial that day the court dismissed the charge against me, saying that Macon's city

100]

council intended to revoke the ordinance against passing out leaflets that had been cited in our arrest there. C. B. asked to be allowed to argue the case, for what if the ordinance were *not* revoked? That would be the end of our challenge to its constitutionality. But his request was denied. We were not to question the council's good faith.

C. B. then took me and Ron to report the outcome to a local Negro who had just started his own small newspaper. The man wanted to use a picture of me and asked an assistant to drive me to a photographer's near by where I could have one taken very quickly. Afterward the assistant asked whether we wanted him to drive us anywhere else. Ron mentioned an errand at the other end of town he wished we had time for, but agreed with me that we didn't have the time—as C. B. would have to wait for us. The assistant misunderstood and drove us there; so C. B. did wait. On our return, he made no complaint. I apologized clumsily, feeling my words inadequate. I couldn't help thinking that *he* would be thinking: she wouldn't have kept a white attorney waiting. Ron had been involved, of course, and he was a Negro too, but I was the older and so responsible.

In the course of the drive home I began to see that the delay had meant more than C. B.'s having to wait for us. It meant that it was dark before we got home, and a Negro man was driving through the dark seated next to a white woman. C. B. was driving fast, to make up the time a little, and the result, ironically, was that he took a wrong turn and lost his route. He had to stop several times to ask directions. He never stopped in any of the places we would have stopped if this had been the North —at a gas station or in the middle of a town at an intersection where a policeman stood: he slowed down only on the outskirts of towns when he could spot in his headlights a Negro walking by the side of the road, and no white man in sight. Glancing at him as he sat next to me at the wheel, concentrated on this trip through the dark—conversing courteously still but his face a mask, composed with obvious discipline—I thought of my eager words to him that morning and the words he had spoken in reply; and I felt in every particle of my being his distance from me.

I was to feel it again, as sharply, on another day. My friends had been in jail about two weeks and were awaiting trial. Brad sent a message out that he needed certain papers to prepare his defense; would I ask C. B. to bring them in to him? Someone else had called to suggest a number of questions I should ask C. B. before the trial. This was Sunday; the trial was set for Tuesday; C. B. could sometimes vanish for a day to appear at court in another town. Afraid of missing him if I waited to call him at his office the next morning, I called him at his home. In a voice that was quiet and courteous and cool, he told me that he did like to reserve Sunday as a day to spend with his family. Again I felt with a pang that perhaps he thought: She wouldn't have disturbed a white attorney. This time I wrote him a note of apology.

I lie now thinking of the constraint there has been between us and of how it has at last dissolved. I think of yesterday, another Sunday. The day before yesterday when C. B. visited, I still felt quite sick, and frightened about myself. Yesterday I woke, feeling better, took a little breakfast, then drowsed off again, and then woke to see C. B. standing there. He was dressed as I had never seen him, in the slacks and loose shirt and slippers he wore about the house. We all sat up in surprise. "I've come to see how Princess Barbara is," he said. I stared at him, not able to find anything to say except that I was better and that it was very good of him to come on Sunday morning—but for once I didn't care if I was awkward.

All the panic I had felt in the past about what he might think, feel, doubt, subsided as he stood there. His words were as usual lightly teasing, but his look put no distance between us. I thought: At last you don't mind our seeing you without a mask. I stared at his face as though I had never seen it before. It seemed suddenly rounder than I had thought it to be, and softer in outline. I thought: Now I dare look at you, too.

Now I sit thinking of how his face flinched when I told him that Yvonne fainted. And the fact that he has shown fear for us suddenly makes the fear that I feel for us myself very much easier to control.

EIGHT

I WAKE from light sleep. For each of us it is becoming harder and harder to sleep for any length of time. We have begun to be able to ignore the almost incessant noise around us and the light in the corridor that burns all night; but now fasting has begun to produce its own wakefulness. On a top berth Edie is awake too, sitting up against the bars, rereading some letters. She leafs through them, the paper rustling. Yvonne turns over, exclaims, "For God's sake, Edie!" "Sorry," Edie says; but several minutes later she lets a number of papers and a pencil drop to the floor. Yvonne exclaims again, then gives up, sits up herself and takes out her copy of Turgenev. Erica alone is undisturbed, just moves one chunky bare foot slightly, without waking. She sleeps dressed in her slip, using her brown cotton wraparound skirt for cover, as a warrior might sleep under his cape—a stolid Spartan figure.

In the distance, two prisoners begin to curse each other. Their voices mount. "Why you—you'd crawl over your two plastered sisters to fuck your own mother, you mother-fucking no-good sonofabitch, why you—"

I get up to get a drink, and then decide to sit on the toilet for a while. It is the only chair in the cell. To sit on the top bunk one has to tuck one's feet under one or let them dangle; to sit up on the lower bunk one has to crouch over with a curved spine; so it is restful here. I also keep hoping that it will be to some purpose. Because I'm

104]

eating very little and get no exercise and because I have no privacy, my bowels have been in a state of paralysis the past sixteen days. It has begun to frighten me a little. I have brought my blanket down from the bunk with me, and now I spread it across my knees, ready to hold it up as a curtain if a guard comes by.

I stare about the cell. Across from me, our night's laundry is draped on the bars—four pairs of underpants, somebody's slip, somebody's bra, a blouse. The things stir slightly in the air, the arms of the blouse gesturing. Suddenly it seems very strange to be here. I begin to indulge myself in comic fantasies. One of these days, I dream, I am bound to explode. My bursting will perhaps burst the bars and the walls of the jail and set all the prisoners free. City officials will be too surprised to act, and my friends will not only walk out of jail—nobody stopping them—but continue their walk through the city, taking now whatever route they want. Soon after this triumph, they will hold a funeral for me, and friends and relatives of mine, and members of the civil rights and peace movements will converge on the city to attend it. Lots of women from W.I.S.P., lots of students from S.N.C.C. Their voices will shake the city of Albany as they all sing: "She could not be moved!"

In the distance the two prisoners have stopped cursing each other and one is making tentative gestures of friendship toward the other. He asks him who he is. "I'm a self-made motherfucker," the second prisoner replies, a little haughtily, "and I lead a pretty good life. I'm temporarily retired."

There is a commotion in the admissions room beyond our cell block. Footsteps in the corridor. I quickly hold up my blanket. Voice of the guard at the door. A woman's voice: "They know damn well I ain't drunk!" The key is noisy in the lock and the heavy steel door grates loudly, swinging open. The woman takes a lurching step across the cell and a pale lost face appears over the top of my blanket. She stares at me in frightened confusion. She swings about, then suddenly exclaims, "There's no room for me in here! The place is all full up!"

Yvonne suggests to the guard that there is an extra mattress on the floor next door; maybe he could move it in here. The guard decides instead to move the woman next door. Our poor friends. The last two people brought in have gone to their cell, too, rather than ours. We hear them all shifting about now to make room for her. Kit is trying to persuade her to take off her shoes, to keep the mattress on the floor as clean as possible; but she is too drunk to understand. She wants a cigarette. It's against the rules to give her one yet; while she is still drunk she might set something on fire. They try to explain. "Just keep your damn cigarettes," she tells them, and she tells them what to do with them.

I climb back up to my bunk with my blanket and pull it up over me. I have the blanket thanks to Ray. He has known that I feel the cold, because on chilly mornings while the Walk was still on the road, I used to carry a hot-water bottle with me. The morning of January 27 when we set out to try again to walk through Albany, he wrapped a pink blanket that belongs to the project around and around his body under his loose Freedom overalls, and an hour or two after we had all been jailed he sent it over to my cell by the run-around. I begin to think about Ray. I remember him that morning, stepping at the head of our line with the lead sign—his tall body oddly flattened and stiffened because of the blanket, but Ray disregarding this and stepping out with a determined sense of his dignity, a rapt concentration on maintaining it under fire. There is a freedom song that has the refrain, "With pride with pride with pride with pride!" and this is how he held himself, the look on his face almost that of a man in a trance.

I lie and wonder how he is doing now. Four days ago he was moved from the Negro "hole," where he and Tyrone Jackson were put after our trial, to a cell by himself next to Brad's in the county jail across the street—or rather, apparently, a cell within Brad's cell. We have had a note from him: "Just a little cage. If I lay catercorner I'll fit. Brad is right beside me, on the runner round of the tiny cage." In another note: "Hey did I tell you girls about our rats? . . . Big! Wow, I thought someone had let a puppy inside of the jail . . . And the roaches . . . I seen a roach carry a whole Biscuit across the floor, picked it up and walked just like a young Mule, what strength, enough for the both of us."

Last Friday morning we had heard him taken—calling out as he was dragged through the large passageway beyond our cells, "Go ahead and kill me!" He has written, "They got very rough with me, but really what is rough? I've been handled like this so long now . . . Dragged on the hard crushed rocks, thrown in the back of the paddy wagon, taken out again, dragged, stomped, kicked, rear end so so sore. . . . So what is rough? . . . I'm really all right, but I have to sit kind of sideways . . . it kind of hurt sitting straight up."

Even before we heard from Ray we had a note from Pete Gregonis about what had happened. Ray and Tyrone had been protesting conditions in the hole, and things had mounted to a violent climax. The hole is filthy and intolerably crowded—though it was even more crowded during the demonstrations Martin Luther King led in 1961. According to Ty, that year as many as seventy or eighty men were sometimes packed into this room, which has triple-decker bunks enough for nine. Now there are twenty-nine men in there—three men to a narrow bunk. At mealtimes the men are herded out into the wide corridor of the cell block to be fed. There are no tables or chairs for them; they sit on the floor or stand. Ray and Ty were let out, too, though they weren't eating; and to protest conditions they began to refuse to walk back into the place. They would sit down in front of one of the cells ranged there—usually the Negro women's cell—and begin to sing freedom songs. The women would join in. The warden or Pritchett would then order the other prisoners from the hole to fetch them. Sometimes Ray would manage to walk right back out while Ty was being brought and would have to be carried in all over again. Pritchett or the warden would order the prisoners not to pick him up but to drag him. Then Friday morning Ray lost control.

It started, according to Pete, when the doctor, making his daily visit, gave an ailing Negro woman prisoner scant attention. Ray began to bang at the shutters in the hole to protest this and ended by breaking shutters and windows. Pete wrote in his log, which he sent over to us: "Suddenly Ray is thrown out of cell. Chief then throws Ray down and almost looks like he is about to pound on Ray. He restrains himself, and Ray is dragged by cops out of sight." Pete has a tendency to moralize; he concludes: "It was unfortunate that the shameful spectacle of windows being broken developed out of what was, at one time, a beautiful protest. We now suffer . . . Pritchett told us he was going to prosecute Ray for damaging city property."

Actually more city property had been damaged than Pete knew: we learned from Ray that he ended by yanking up the toilet by its roots and setting it by the door. Ray wrote us: "I will try to explain . . . I pull it up for attention . . . I did not trust my nonviolence. I know if I did something like this, Chief Pritchett would find a

108]

place for me, probably the county jail . . . I believe if I had stay in the hole with all of those people I would've become more and more angry. But the main reason is because I didn't want to see Barbara Deming and Yvonne Klein taken out to go to the hospital. Yes, I want them to get treatment, but I think Dr. Hilsman and Pritchett have wait too long with these two. They playing a game and this game can be very serious . . . I know I will get charge with destroying city property . . . I would rather be charge with this than be charge with hitting Pritchett or one of his police officers. I know when I taken about all the harassment I possibly can take. Pritchett become very hostile toward me. And by his knowing my background, he has started picking on this to provoke me into a fight. I say now, I don't *think* I'll fight back at him. I don't think. But if one of those people die or ruins their health, I really don't know what I'll do . . . By knowing myself I prefer solitary to make sure."

Pete is literally correct that Ray's action was "unfortunate"; it will certainly complicate our lives now. But I think that he very probably did keep himself, this way, from doing worse. And I think of what he has written in this note, and of the meaning of it. "If one of these people die, or ruins their health, I really don't know what I'll do . . ." I think of Ray when he first joined the Walk. Sometimes when we passed through small towns that were particularly hostile, he would put dark glasses on— so that people could not see the look in his eyes, he explained; he couldn't help looking hate at them. Sometimes he would also put his glasses on during the meetings we'd hold among ourselves at the start or the end of a day. A number of times I begged him to take them off: "It's hard to talk with you; I don't know where you are." But he obviously didn't want us to know. He was still full of suspicion of us—not at all sure that we were really in

[109

the same fight that he was. I remember him one day standing in a corner with Yvonne, his eyes blazing, his voice like a whip flailing at her: "You people make me sick!" He had one particular grievance at first: for some time after we entered the South we had only a leaflet that spoke of our concern with U.S.-Cuban relations, no words on paper about how we felt about discrimination. We had felt that we hardly needed to put this on paper, when people could see us walking down the road together, but Ray was right that it was better to put it in words too—as we finally did. I remember a look he turned on me one day. He had argued in several meetings that the small group that talked with local officials before the Walk arrived in a town should be integrated, no matter how provocative this might be—or what were we walking for? Most of us opposed such a policy as reckless, and I was among these; but in one town, Athens, Georgia, we decided to make the experiment, and Ray went along on the visit to the chief of police. The meeting was without incident. On his return, Ray walked up to me. I can't remember his words, because the look he gave me shook the words themselves out of my head, but the gist of his question was: had his presence been so disastrous? He didn't have his dark glasses on, but as he stared at me, his eyes were themselves so blackly glazed with bitterness that I couldn't look into them, couldn't see beyond their shiny surface. I was angry myself at this assault, and told him so and turned away.

It was most often at Bradford that Ray would take offense. Partly because Bradford had a special eagerness to see the Walk reach Cuba, and not come to a stop in one jail after another in the South; whereas the Walk had reality for Ray only in the South. Partly because, simply, they are such opposite temperaments. I think: How strange it is to have them sitting there now in adjoining solitary cages—"the big two," Ray jokes (he partly jokes, partly doesn't joke). Bradford dedicated to sobriety and the way of reason, which seems to him quite possible to attain if one will school oneself: "Friends, all things proceed by certain laws . . ." Ray dedicated to no such thing: "Oh it is wonderful to write from the heart and not all from the mind. Altho the mind is involved. I feel like blowing soul. I have quite a bit to blow." Brad pledged to a difficult self-discipline—to abstinence, to celibacy, to vegetarianism. Ray: "Man, when I drink wine, I don't sip it!" No one is supposed to touch liquor while we are in the South, but Ray has on a number of occasions done more than sip it even here, to Brad's great distress.

Yet more, perhaps, makes these two alike than makes them unlike. Both of them very much alone, both of them clumsy in their loneliness, but also very often eloquent—in the words they speak and in the gestures that they make—because the same feeling that what they are doing is altogether necessary grips them both, painfully. This calling impelled Brad, about eight years before, to abandon a successful business career and enter the non-violent movement full time; it has impelled Ray, a shorter time ago, to abandon a life of drifting. I think of how he used to feel toward us—remember him at so many of our meetings, on his feet suddenly, his head stretched forward on his long neck as he jabbed at us with his words—and I think of his words now, in that note. I think of another note he has written recently, to Brad: "I very very proud to be among all of you, not because you a bunch of whites but because you the kind of people I've been trying to find a long long time, and now I've found youse and don't know how to respond because I just don't know how, I guess I've been searching too long to meet you, and now since I found you I don't know how to cope with you."

[111

I think: Yes, and we have been searching to find you; it seems a long time, too; and we don't know how to cope, either.

And then I begin to think of Ray and of Chief Pritchett. The Chief does plan to prosecute Ray, and he has been around to say so, announcing it with as much pleasure as he had announced his success in breaking Ray's water fast. I think of the very particular struggle that has taken place between these two. Ray has obsessed the Chief's imagination from the start. He has, for one thing, been especially uncooperative—even flipping himself off the stretcher as he was being carried into jail. Just the fact of his great physical strength and agility has obsessed the Chief, giving him hope of provoking him into using it to our discredit—especially when he learned that Ray had once been a professional boxer. Then, not long after the first arrest, he discovered that Ray had a police record. I suppose he made inquiries about us through the F.B.I., hoping for something to use against us. Ray had been charged a number of times with drunkenness and also with assault. When I walked into the police station after Pritchett had discovered this, I found all the cops in a state of boyish excitement. They told me to watch the Albany *Herald* closely; there would be a story soon that I mustn't miss. Pritchett turned his facts over to the editor, who gave them prominent space immediately.

I lie and think about this first in a series of "victories" the Chief has scored over Ray—and over all of us through Ray. He had hoped to discredit us by publicly "exposing" Ray, but there had followed from his action a much more thorough exposure of Ray's character than he expected. I had asked Ray whether he would like to write any kind of a statement in reply to the charges, and he had written: "Yes I was one of the angry young men, yes I rebel against society. I had no respect for law and order or man, espe-

112]

cially the white man the one who has made me feel inferior . . . The most powerful weapon to me at the time being hatred, disrespect for anyone [white], I never trusted him, and every chance I got, I tried to hurt him . . . I was violence. I got at one point where I started waiting for one to assault me, where I could strike back with all my strength . . . I could not fight him legally, and win, so I decided to take up boxing where the world could watch and see me beat one with my hands . . . Revenge was what I thought I got . . . So now come a new thing to me that's called nonviolence and I'm trying it. But yet my past of hatred for him has been stirred up again. Which way shall I go? It's easy to go back to revenge, and God know I have all the rights . . . This thing that's called nonviolence is the biggest challenge I have ever tried as a man and altho it's hard, I have manage to continue to hold my violence in check. But how much longer can I stay this way? . . . Maybe more strength on my part will help. But really why should it be on my part, especially since I the oppressed. I'll just leave things into God's hands. But here I'm confused about God, where is he *now*? I need him *now*. But just when do God put his hand into this thing? . . . God . . . can't you see just what I going thru as a young man? If I sound as tho I'm beginning to doubt you, God, if there's one, show me your face, don't keep hiding your face from me, don't put words into others' mouths to explain to me about you . . . But yet God I haven't thrown you completely out of my mind. So give me strength and courage to continue onward to things unknown, who knows what the tomorrows will bring."

I had sent a copy of this statement to the editor of the *Herald* and asked whether he would agree to publish it in the letter column. To my surprise he printed it in its entirety. We also mimeographed copies to pass out at a mass meeting the Albany Movement was to hold. A day or so before the meeting I showed it to the secretary of the Movement, Mr. Page. An older man with an extensive knowledge of Albany, he had come to our headquarters to help us compile a list of influential white citizens. We wanted to mail them an explanation of why we were struggling with the city authorities. He was very helpful to us that day and happy to talk about those who held power here, warning us: "They are relentless; I can't emphasize that too much." He was full of tales and advice. It was also perfectly clear that he felt reluctant to have the Albany Movement identify itself with us. I showed him Ray's statement and he read it through, slowly. He said, "It's a prayer," and then he sat for a long time, silent- his brow wrinkled now, and something working in his eyes. He said very little more, except to ask whether he could take a copy away with him. At the meeting he read Ray's words aloud, with emotion. He still made no recommendation that the Albany Movement take action in support of ours; but it was obvious that he no longer felt remote from us.

I wonder now whether the words published in the *Herald* could have touched any of the paper's readers in the white community. It doesn't seem impossible to me. I wonder how they have affected Pritchett himself. Even before they appeared in print, a friend of the project, a Negro woman active in the Mennonite church in Atlanta —who has known Pritchett in the past and has managed to gain his respect—called him and read Ray's statement to him over the telephone. Ray had now begun his first water fast, and she had arrived in Albany, in response to a call from me, to be of what help she could. She told me that after she read Ray's words to the Chief there was simply a long silence at the other end of the line. The Chief could usually find something to say, and it was her guess—though it could only be a guess—that he had been shaken. I ask myself: To what degree is the Chief still able to believe his own descriptions of the kind of person Ray is? For from the start both Pritchett and the other cops have loved to stand outside our cell telling us what a really violent, what a frightening man Ray is—really more beast than man, they have implied.

I remember suddenly an incident Ray has described in a note he sent us after Pritchett scared him into breaking his second water fast by sending him to the psychiatric ward of the hospital. "I never thought of being threaten with a bug house. But I shouldn't let even that worry me. But I did . . . I was just plain scare, yes scare . . . I know I wouldn't live two hours in a nut house down here." While he was held there, one of the cops we knew well was assigned to guard him in his room. The cop grew terribly sleepy as the night wore on, and Ray suggested that he lie down on the other bed in the room and take a nap; Ray would keep watch and wake him if anyone came. The cop removed his heavy belt with its decorated pistol in a holster and hung it on the bedpost and stretched out in the bed next to Ray's and slept "like a baby" until morning. I remind myself now that in that childishly trusting act, he acknowledged his contradictory and most real sense of Ray's nature. I remind myself, too, of the Chief's surprising act upon Ray's return—when he brought around to my cell some writings Ray wanted me to see. Would he have been moved to such a gesture if, in the course of gaining his "victory" over Ray, Ray had not become for him the opposite of the grotesque stereotype the Chief liked to conjure up for us—if he had not become for him a real person?

Ray wrote to us about breaking his fast, "I chicken out and Pritchett won again," but I think to myself, You won, too. Perhaps the very fact that Ray has to struggle with himself more than most to try to be nonviolent has made him especially real to a man like Pritchett. Remembering the Chief's excitement when he came around to announce to us that Ray had wrecked the hole, I think: He is trying to forget now what he has come to see in Ray, but his elation is forced. Then suddenly I ask myself: Or am I deceiving myself—hoping for something against hope?

NINE

I FALL asleep, exhausted, and dream:
I am on a mountainside and I fly off onto the branch of a large oak tree and sit there for a while, getting my breath, trying to be calm. Suddenly I feel alarm about my friends. At this, I find myself abruptly at the base of the mountain. Someone is telling me that my friends are high up the mountainside and in trouble. I begin to try to hurry up the slope to them, but I find that the steep ground is slippery and I slide back again and again. I can't think what to do until the idea comes to me to spread on the slope the blanket Ray has given me. I spread it out carefully and it covers the slope and I find that by falling on my hands and knees I can creep slowly up . . .

I wake. My friends are passing around another joint letter to the men.

Yvonne has written: "Dear Troglodites—I have been asleep for some days now, but when I wake up I think about you. For Ralph especially: fresh mushroom soup (not canned, not cream of), Quiche Lorraine, a salad with three kinds of lettuce . . . For Marv: a large slice of halvah . . ."

Edie has written: "Dear masterly men, I can only suggest gingerbread with thick hot lemon sauce, and that fools rush out . . . Oh, love . . . P.S.: All reports to the contrary, I remain disgustingly healthy."

Kit has written: "Dear wonderful fellows, I write to correct what seems to me a terrible error. Gingerbread cannot be eaten with lemon sauce! . . . I've been growing weaker daily . . . Do you get hot flashes when you start to black out on standing up? . . . Are your spirits high and soaring? Isn't *anyone* near collapse? . . ."

And Mary: "Dear People, I keep saying that gingerbread is best with lemon sauce *or* whipped cream . . ."

Michele writes: "Dear ones—Love, love . . . Tomatoes are in season now; peaches soon; oranges, grapefruits. *Figs* . . . I'm pretty impressed with my strength. Everyone else is weakening promisingly . . ."

As they are writing, Clarence, the run-around, arrives with some notes from the men. There are notes from Brad and Ray included. C. B. by mistake, left them with the men yesterday instead of with us.

Gene Keyes writes: "Dearest Pipestemmes . . . We heard you singing last night, bravo . . . I write humbled and speechless at your stamina, and will wind up now with no thoughts more profound than maple sugar. Oh, maybe some buttered noodles—and love again."

Pete Gregonis writes: ". . . If I had a blender I could whip you up such delights like a drink I call 'avocado ecstasy' . . ."

Ray writes: "My beautiful Family of Women! . . . After reading your wonderful letters, I must say now, oh it is great to be working (playing) with you for humanity sake!"

Brad writes simply: "Ladies—Whenever I think of your courage and patience my spirit is raised and will strengthened."

I think of the family that we have become. There are those of us who are of such very different disposition that we have found ourselves endlessly capable of irritating one another—especially on the road together, at the beginning or the end of a day, crowded again into the basement of a Negro church where we have been given permission to spread our sleeping bags and hold our strategy

118]

meetings; interminable meetings, because we try to be absolutely democratic and each person is allowed to voice dissent until satisfied, even if this wears away the hours we have to sleep, which some of us need more than others. Perhaps in the early mornings we have tried each other most, all of us tense, not knowing what the day will bring, and each of us having his own way of preparing himself. Ray, upon arising, for example, liked to put a recording of *Green Onions* on the Walk's portable record player and stretch out his long limbs in a few concentrated dance steps; Brad, sitting taut upright in his sleeping bag, liked to be allowed to collect his thoughts silently. Some of us liked to drive out quietly to the spot on the highway where we would begin to walk; some liked to gather their courage by singing at the top of their lungs. And then a few of us liked to try to keep our headquarters in some kind of order, while most others happily created about them an almost absolute disorder. Each of us has his own way of talking to strangers and officials, and there is a good deal of competitiveness among us here. When a cop visits this cell now, for instance, Erica sometimes accuses Edie of doing too much of the talking, while Edie feels that Erica, when she speaks up, is not as subtle as she, Edie, knows how to be. We have annoyed each other daily, but even before we entered jail together we have begun, too, to feel bound to one another in an extraordinary way. A kind of affection flows between us that I have known before only on other ventures like this—born in part of enduring together discomfort and danger (I have read often that soldiers can feel for each other a love that is altogether special in their lives), and born of one thing more, too: our common attempt to act toward our antagonists with sympathy. This daily effort, however clumsy, to put from us not only our fear of them but our hostility draws us closer still, as we reveal ourselves to one

[119

another, disarmed and hopeful. I have never felt toward a group of people a love so sweet and so strange. The emotion of it is as sharp as though I were in love with each of them. It is a physical love: before we were jailed, when we drove out each morning to the place on the highway where we had stopped walking the day before, it was always welcome to me that we were packed into the cars tightly, our bodies thrown against each other. But it is not a possessive love. It has astonished me to feel so sharp an affection that was not. And what most astonishes me is to love so intensely so many people at the same time.

There are moments now when to feel this love seems literally to sweeten the rancid air we breathe and to enlarge our cell without limit and to illumine it, so that I stare at the shadows the bars cast across the newspapers we have spread on the floor and think how beautiful this place is, and I am filled with a peculiar well-being, a feeling both gay and grave. And there are other times when it is too much for me to feel toward them as I do. I remember the day, soon after our trial, when Pritchett gave the eight women who had been living in one cell the choice of splitting up—some of us moving into the adjoining cell. Four of us moved, and it was only logical, for the crowding had been hard on all of us; but I remember with surprise still how very difficult it was to make the decision. I remember throwing myself down on a bunk all to myself. The freedom to stretch out was a pleasure that was acute, but more acute still was the feeling of having been torn from the four next door—though we were right next to each other and could still talk freely and pass things back and forth. The wall between us seemed hardly endurable. I remember the moment when Yvonne fell, and how I had felt in a frightening way as though I were falling myself. And I remember, too, the morning when Ray was dragged off to the county jail. Someone shouted,

"They're taking Ray!" I was lying flat on my back on a lower bunk, still weak from illness. I heard Ray calling out and then I heard the sound of his long body dragged across the cement floor of the passageway beyond our cells; and then with astonishment I felt the shock of the rough cement against the length of my own body. I turned my head to the wall and began to weep—it had startled me so to feel as though there were no distinction at all between his body and mine.

I try to think about this peculiar love which I have come to feel for all of them—and which they, obviously, experience too. If we can hope to win something in the struggle in which we are engaged, it is perhaps above all with this love-for-more-than-one that we are armed. By it we lend one another strength to be stubborn. Because of it our antagonists must find us surprisingly indivisible. And the contagion of it, its overspilling, makes it more possible for us to act with that sympathy for them which could help to make them reconsider their resistance to what we ask.

To feel within me a sympathy for others very much more free and active than usual is a little intoxicating. I wonder what the limits are to such sympathy, and how much it might be able to bring about—and how much it has brought about already, in history. I think suddenly of a passage in Amitai Etzioni's *The Hard Way to Peace*. He has been trying to define what order, when it exists, is based upon, and he has said that its only real foundation is a sense of moral community among men, some degree of willing commitment on their part not to use violence against one another when they differ; for no government, otherwise, ever has enough power to control men. And then he has made the observation that stirred my imagination: the scope of the community of those who feel this commitment to one another has gradually expanded

[121

throughout history, to include more and more men beyond local borders and to include more and more groups within a particular society, once considered alien. I muse again about the way this has come about. Couldn't one say that as exploration, conquest, trade, invention have gradually thrown more and more men's lives closely together, it has become steadily more necessary—if their lives were to have any serenity—to begin to trust themselves to one another a little and treat one another as somehow kin, whatever their differences? This acknowledgment of kinship has always lagged behind the necessity for it, and at this point of history the lag is terrifying. But the human gift that has made it possible for men to commit themselves to one another even to the degree that they have, the gift that has made life possible at all (and now makes it possible, though not inevitable, that life on this earth will continue)—isn't it that ability to cast out fear of others and recognize one's essential likeness to them, that I feel within myself now in surprisingly active form? Might not history well be rewritten in terms of the operation, faltering but persistent, of this more than personal spirit of sympathy?

I think: how flickering it is in all of us, how little under our control. I can feel this in myself, and I remember, too, how often as a group we have let its force be deflected. I can remember times when, absorbed entirely by one another, celebrating among ourselves the feelings between us, we have almost ignored those who were giving us hospitality for the night, or, when the route was not dangerous, almost ignored those whom we passed on the road— just because we felt there was something extraordinary about this love between us, intoxicated by it; at which it ceased to be extraordinary and we became, toward our hosts, mere locust swarms descending, and for those who have watched us pass, merely a fantastic parade. Sometimes we have ignored in the same way one or another of our own group, clumsier than others, less able to sustain this very special rapport.

I remind myself that all the great religions have recognized the creative power of love; but in every established church the attempt to live by it has deteriorated into a celebration of the fact that a few people feel they are the initiated, and one of the most difficult labors is to persist in trying to break open and enlarge the charmed circle of sympathies that already exist.

My thoughts are interrupted. Yvonne and Erica are having an argument about something. Erica has just declared, "It stands to reason."

"Oh really, Erica!" Yvonne exclaims.

"Yes, really, Erica!" Edie agrees with Yvonne. "You make things sound so much simpler than they are."

Yvonne adds, "Someday I would like to have you explain to me just what you mean by 'reason.' The longer I live, the less it means to *me*."

Erica stares at first one and then the other of them, bewildered.

TEN

Yvonne has been force-fed. At midmorning she was led upstairs to trial—at last—looking very shaky on her legs, and she was given fifteen days. Then about one o'clock two cops came to tell her that they were taking her to the hospital. They took me along, too, to be given blood tests and a series of enemas. Pritchett has learned to cut expenses: we were taken back and forth not in the ambulance that was used during the first jail-in, but simply in a squad car.

It was strange to emerge into daylight. After our bare cell, the world seemed there in bewildering detail, and I found it hard to focus my eyes. One of the streets we drove down was lined with live oaks. "Look! All the trees have leaves now!" Yvonne exclaimed—forgetting that live oaks, as one of the cops drily reminded her, kept their leaves all the year round; and forgetting too, of course, that spring is still a long way off. But it *was* a little as though a new season had arrived, transforming the world, which had been without color or motion—brightening it abruptly. The unaccustomed light of day dazzled us, and every leaf on every tree glittered. I had not quite realized how little daylight falls into the narrow alley outside our cells and then filters to us through the dirty windows across the corridor. I had done my best one day to clean the windows. When Yvonne was jailed before the rest of us, Edie had brought her knitting to her (Pritchett, to our surprise, had allowed her to keep it), and by tying a wad of wet toilet paper to one of the long knitting needles and reaching out as far as I could through the bars, first with my arm, later with a leg, the contraption tied to my foot, I had cleared a certain area of glass—which made a difference, but not the difference I had hoped. In the hospital emergency room to which Yvonne and I were assigned now and told to undress and put on hospital gowns, I stared at my clothes as I took them off. I had thought I was managing to keep fairly clean, but suddenly in the brightly lit room everything I had on looked gray. We were left alone for a while and, while Yvonne lay down, I tried walking all about the room, slowly. At the first steps I had taken, outside the cell, I had felt that I had to learn all over again how to put one foot in front of the other. Again the world seemed all new. To walk! I felt as changed as though I had found that I could fly.

Two nurses finally took me off to another room. They obviously knew who we were and were very curious about us, but when I asked them whether they saw any sense in what we were doing or whether it just seemed crazy to them, one of them answered quickly—in alarm—that they'd rather not talk about it; what they thought had nothing to do with the role they had to play here. So we talked about nursing for a while. They were both very friendly during this discussion, and very gentle with me throughout—young women, both of them, one a regular nurse and the other, very pretty, still in training. Then at a certain point, to explain my state, I began to talk about the lack of privacy in jail. They were curious about jail and listened eagerly. Soon I was able to talk about how hard things were for Yvonne. And suddenly one of them asked, "You're not thinking of giving up?" I said we believed very much in what we were doing. She answered that some of the people in this city also believed in what *they* were doing, and I agreed that of course it was so.

Then the other asked, with a shy but eager look on her face, "Do you find Albany difficult?" I told her that yes, we did find it difficult—we had had no such struggle in any other city; and they both looked pleased and proud.

I was still in the room with Yvonne, however, when she was force-fed. Doctor Hilsman seemed a little more friendly than usual today; he had a cigarette in his hand when he came in and he and Yvonne began to discuss the dangers of smoking. He gave her intravenous feeding first, as he had done when she was brought to the hospital toward the end of the first jail term. From the bed next to hers I watched with relief the yellow sugar water bubbling down the tube that dangled above her. She was out of danger. Then the doctor tried to give her orange juice through a tube in her nose. Now that I am back in the cell again, I keep remembering it—watching again, in shock, from the next bed, unable to help her.

He couldn't seem to force the tube into place. I watched her legs writhe convulsively, as he argued with her, "Why don't you just agree to drink it?" He was flustered and couldn't understand why she was stubborn. She was crying now, helplessly; but she wouldn't agree. She was shaking her head from side to side, struggling against him. He had set a hypodermic tube on the foot of the bed and, thrashing with her legs, she kicked it off the bed and it shattered on the floor. "I didn't mean to do that; I'm sorry," she told him—almost angrily. She asked him to give her a few minutes to get hold of herself, and he left the room—relieved, himself, I think, to stop for a while. I went to sit beside her and she told me, "I feel as though he's breaking me into pieces!" There was blood on her face. I wondered: When is this going to end for her?

I try to stop thinking about it now. It finally occurred to the doctor to try a smaller tube. Then he fed her

126]

orange juice that he had taken straight from the refrigerator; the ice-cold impact of it on her empty stomach left her stunned for several hours. As we rode back to jail together in the squad car, she sat staring in front of her, not even thinking to wipe away the tears in her eyes.

Nobody in either cell has spoken for some time now; we are all feeling very sober. There has been eager talk before this about reaching the point when the authorities will have to begin taking one of us after another off to the hospital to be fed, for then things will begin to be most complicated for the city; but that eagerness has been tempered—everyone knows now what the experience can be. It will vary, probably, for different people, but each of my friends now faces the possibility that it will be the torture that it was for Yvonne.

ELEVEN

I AM SITTING on a top bunk with Edie, because a new-comer is in the lower bunk I have been using. She was brought in this afternoon, very drunk—a dejected young woman, skinny legs in tapered slacks, naked breasts under her loose gray cardigan sweater; she collapsed on the bunk and is still sleeping it off. Every now and then she belches loudly in her sleep or she breaks wind; the sour air of our cell turns still more sour. It is the hour when more and more prisoners begin to be pulled in off the streets, and their tirades against the police, their calls back and forth, again bombard us. I have made a habit of writing down in a notebook what they call out, but to-night I try not to hear them. I would like suddenly to yell myself—to yell at all of them to shut up and let me for-get their weakness; to yell for a cop to come and take away the woman who has my bed, so that I can fall asleep and forget about my own weakness and that of my friends. I lean against the bars and try to think about the past two days. I am afraid that our struggle is about to end, and in defeat.

Yesterday Pritchett allowed us to hold a group meet-ing. A. J. Muste told him that he could not continue to negotiate on our behalf without such a meeting with us all—with no cops present—so Pritchett let us gather in the very wide corridor outside the cells in the larger cell block. A. J. and Dave Dellinger were both present, and also two others from the group working for us outside,

Carl and Allen. And C. B. was there. There was some question as to whether or not the Chief would allow Ray to attend, but he finally decided to. Ray and Brad were brought from across the street, and the rest of us, from our various cells, filed in—slow-motion, on weak legs—and embraced frailly and peered into one another's faces, trying to gauge what strength we still had.

On each face the cost of all these days was written plainly. I had watched the women change hour by hour and so grown a little accustomed to it; the change in some of the men was a shock. John-i-thin could hardly speak. Tony—who once had such a look of impudent youth about him, one of the boldest in the group (we had to restrain him and Kit from dropping in on the Klan meeting the evening of the day their sound truck drew alongside of us on the road near Athens)—Tony looked now like a little anxious thin-lipped old man, nervously fingering the scraggly goatee he had grown. I stared at Brad, too: his eyes burned as though he had a fever; his lips, like Tony's, were paper thin, and his smile, when he smiled, was a fixed grimace. His face had a painful rigidity, as though all his good humor had wasted from him and there remained only intellect and stubbornly set will. It was not even only those who were fasting who were changed. Peter and Eric and Michael, who had been eating all along, looked drained of health, too; the airless cramped confinement had been enough. I saw Dave Dellinger moving among the prisoners. Dave had been in here himself for about a week; he keeps turning up whenever we seem to need reinforcement, and he was one of the seven people arrested toward the end of the first jail-in. He is familiar enough with the effects of a long fast—as a C.O. in the Second World War he fasted sixty-five days to win reforms in the prison where he was held. But as I approached him I saw a look of struggle on his face; his chin began to tremble; he told me, "When I see you, I just can't help crying." As we hugged, a queer little rippling explosion of sobs burst from him for a moment, and then he recovered his calm.

We all sat down on some filthy mattresses dragged from the nearby cells (Pritchett doesn't seem to have given everybody mattress covers), and A. J. opened the meeting, describing to us how negotiations had been going: "I can't give you an optimistic report." A series of mailings had been sent out—to the local community, to news media, to people throughout the country who might possibly write or act in our behalf—trying to make clear the issues we saw involved (analyses Brad had written, a letter Kit had sent out from jail, the statement I had made in court, appeals written by Dave and others); a series of meetings had taken place with city officials; but the few tentative hopes that had been held for a while had now faded. An anonymous businessman of Albany, a certain "Mr. X," had come forward to suggest a compromise solution, but the authorities had not been interested. The mayor in one interview had suggested that the city manager, Stephen Roos, might have authority to reach an agreement with us on his own, and not have to ask for a vote among the city commissioners; this had made A. J. hopeful for a while, but Roos by now had made it clear that he felt he had no such leeway, and he had emphasized to A. J. and Dave the solidarity of the commissioners where we were concerned: it was "Oglethorpe or nothing"—we could walk down that street or we could go on sitting in jail.

A. J. had pointed out to various officials that the longer the walkers were held in jail on an issue of civil liberties, the closer they and the Albany Movement were drawn together, by just that issue. Already the Movement had

130]

come out with published statements in support of our stand. A student group that had been formed because of impatience with the general inaction of the older leaders had written, "It has been rumored that the Negroes of Albany are not 100% behind the Peace and Freedom Walkers. If you are a victim of this thinking, the President and members of the Albany Student Movement have a surprise for you. We fully support their right to express their beliefs . . . and will assist them in any way we can . . ." Pritchett was obviously impressed by the possibilities of trouble here, A. J. reported, but he still gave no sign at all of readiness to grant us what we asked. And, of course, a number of people remarked, whether or not the Albany Movement would really begin to give the city trouble again it was impossible to predict. There were rumors of it sometimes, but they were very vague.

Dave next gave his report on the publicity that had been given to our struggle. There had been very, very little. He himself considered it to be a key battle that we were fighting, but on the whole even those people up North he would have expected to be especially aware of our situation and active on our behalf tended, when he spoke about us, to ask, "Oh, are they still in jail?" A cruel fact was that what newspaper mention of us there was failed usually even to note that we were fasting. He wasn't saying that there could not still be a newsbreak that would at last make what we were doing visible to the country, but we must not expect it. "I only say this with anguish," he told us. From the point of view of the long-run erosion of the power structure here, he believed that our stand was of great value; but from the point of view of any decisive breakthrough we might achieve, he could offer us little hope. And what he and A. J. had to know now was whether we wanted to persist nevertheless, and serve

[131

out our sentences, while they continued to negotiate for us as best they could, or whether we wanted to call the battle off.

The discussion that followed was long-drawn-out, as discussion always is among us. It proceeded more slowly than usual, because some people found their words with difficulty, and when they did find them they were often hard to hear. Everybody was tense. Brad would interject, "It's inconsiderate to the group if you don't speak up." Ray would slap his knee with his hand and sarcastically interject for the one who had mumbled, "Okay, Brad!" Somewhere in the middle of the meeting, John-i-thin had to be helped to a bunk in one of the cells; he couldn't sit up any longer.

As always the responses among us differed widely. Erica was for serving out our sentences, if it came to that, and then resting for a brief period before deciding whether or not to confront the authorities a third time. Perhaps most people would decide we hadn't the strength for a third time, but she believed in leaving that decision open: we should never shut off possibilities that lay in the future—as we should not at this point panic and shut off the possibility, however slight, that the authorities would decide to concede to us. "Beautiful, Erica," said Ray. Hers was the boldest suggestion made. Kit was reluctant to consider a third confrontation, but, she said, the fast would begin to put maximum pressure on the authorities only when a number of people began to be force-fed; four or five of us would probably have to be taken to the hospital within the coming week, so we should wait and see what happened after this. Two of the men in the terribly crowded and filthy hole now spoke up for calling an end to the struggle here, if hopes were so slim, and turning the project back into a Walk again. But Tony objected; he agreed with Kit that when more people started going to the hospital the picture could change. Barry Bassin suggested a compromise: we could make some new proposals to the city and give ourselves another week or ten days to wait for their acceptance.

At this point Brad sat up very straight and began to try to rouse the group to make a general decision to serve out our sentences. At the start of the meeting he had been apprehensive that a lot of us might want to consider a third attempt to walk through Albany; he was afraid we would never be on our way to Cuba again. But now he was afraid we would be too quick to leave the city. As we had already engaged ourselves in this present battle, he urged us to steel ourselves to persist in it. He gave a short lecture on the methods historically used to break men's wills. We should refuse to let our wills be broken. He urged those who felt ready to surrender to lighten their loads, to break their fasts if they had to, but to stay in jail—for ("all projects are governed by laws") the longer we stayed in jail the more pressure we put on the city and the more chance there was that we could win something. Those who couldn't stick it any longer at all should bail out, rather than arguing that others should quit.

Yvonne, too, was for persisting—though it was hard for her to speak, she said, because her sentence was shorter than some. But she told Brad that she disliked the *way* in which he had spoken. She didn't want anyone to be moved simply by rhetoric to stick it out—and then to find himself terribly unhappy. And nobody should be stampeded into thinking that Brad's was the only honorable proposal. Others interjected, too, that some might be for quitting not because they felt incapable of sticking it out but simply because they disagreed that anything could be gained by it.

It was hard for me to speak, too, but I said it seemed to me that even if we won no visible concessions by persisting, we should consider the long-term gains there were to be won—as people both in this community and elsewhere looked back on our action and weighed its meaning. And I put forward my proposal that if when we got out of jail we were still refused permission to walk out of town on any route but Oglethorpe, we should walk down Oglethorpe handing out a new leaflet, and it should ask the people of Albany to consider whether their refusal to grant us our rights did not constitute a defeat for them as much as for us.

But a number of voices were raised again for quitting now or soon. Edie's was. She thought we had done what we could. Alan's was. Eric's was—not because things were rough in the hole. He had said before we walked into Albany that we should spend no more than thirty days in any battle here; he thought we had already taken too much time out.

Brad, seeing how many for one reason or another were reluctant to serve out the sentences, now took up Barry's suggestion that we should persist for a limited number of days. One thing that troubled all of us was that some people had not even been sentenced yet; the noncooperators had not, and Ray had not been tried on the charge of destroying city property. If we called the struggle off as of a certain date, there was a better chance that the city would want to release us all together. Brad suggested March 1 as a cutoff date. Yvonne was due to get out on that day, some of us on March 5, some of us on March 15. "It weakens the struggle fifteen days at the most."

A long discussion followed as to what would be the best date. Many preferred an earlier one. As this question was labored, I sat there confused, feeling blind depression grow in me. I was too exhausted to be able to analyze my anxiety; I just sat, staring at the emaciated faces of my friends, staring about the cell block, beginning to listen

134]

to the occasional sounds of the cops beyond the door and beyond the shuttered window into the admissions room.

At a certain point in the discussion Barry suddenly asked if we would announce to the authorities that we planned to persist for a set number of days only. Because if we did, he couldn't see that we would be putting much pressure on them. Brad thought that the added days and the publicity they might bring as people went off to the hospital could make them very unhappy; but others agreed with Barry: What date we chose was really quite arbitrary. Edie declared, "I would prefer something like tomorrow—which would have symbolism, too: it's St. Valentine's Day."

At this Erica suddenly rose up on her knees with a kind of jumping motion, as if startled out of sleep. She said it was clear that setting a terminal date involved us in serious problems, and she would like us to reconsider the whole question of whether to set such a date or not. Everybody stared at this, for it was now late in the afternoon and we had seemed on the point of reaching a group decision, and a few people began to object. But Dave backed her up, warning that we shouldn't make any decisions, under pressure of time, that we might be unhappy with later. I looked up and saw Pritchett standing in the doorway, surveying us. Dave informed him that we all needed to mull over some of the things we had been talking about and then perhaps to have another very short meeting together. The Chief nodded and told us we were due back in our cells. Everybody seemed to me a little dazed as we filed out of the room.

That evening the Chief visited our cell. He looked very ruddy and boyish and pleased with life. He was in mufti and wearing some new very pale pigskin-colored lounging shoes. He told us that he was leaving for a vacation in Nassau on the sixteenth and wouldn't be back until the twenty-second; he hoped we wouldn't make any decisions while he was away. Then he smiled broadly. He told us he had had a tape recorder hidden in the room during our meeting and he had just finished listening to it. He liked best Edie's idea about leaving the next day, St. Valentine's Day.

We all should have taken it for granted that he would listen in on the "private" meeting he had granted us. We knew our phones were tapped at the office, knew that he had spies at all the mass meetings. I remembered the growing uneasiness I had felt as we talked, and I couldn't understand why I hadn't been able to put a name to it. We had a long tradition, of course, of open meetings. We frequently laid our plans with police officials sitting in or standing near, and this worked to our advantage, for it reduced their suspicions of us; we wanted, after all, to establish trust between us. But in this instance hadn't we helped them not only to trust us but to trust us not to give them any further trouble worth the name? It was one thing to reveal to them quite openly some immediate action we planned; it was another to reveal just the degree of strength and determination we had left for further action. Now I feel disgust with myself that I hadn't been alert enough to raise this question at the start of the meeting—to point out that we undoubtedly *were* overheard, and suggest that at a certain point we should perhaps poll the attitudes of the group in writing. It seems to me that we have so weakened our position that unless there is a real change of feeling among us and a decision to serve out our sentences, we *would* do better to quit now; for by persisting just a short time, the authorities well aware of how long that time would be, what pressure can we put on them that would justify asking Yvonne to go through force feeding again, asking others to go through it and perhaps have just as hard a time? About an hour ago I heard a Negro woman prisoner as she was brought into a cell cry out, "Oh, peacewalkers, help!" So *someone* still thinks there is some power in us; but I am afraid, myself, that we have let it slip from us.

The day has passed without decision. Early this morning the Chief appeared again. Edie was sleeping and he gave a little tug at her hair to wake her up. Then he told us that we'd be having a second meeting at one o'clock; this time he would chair the discussions and we would make up our minds. (Everybody laughed aloud at that.) One o'clock has passed, though; the afternoon has passed, and neither the Chief nor one of his men nor A. J. nor C. B. has appeared, either to summon us to a meeting or to give us any news. We have exchanged a few valentines with each other, through Clarence, the run-around. Marv has sent a note that he is breaking his fast—"for love of his stomach." And we have endlessly discussed what happened yesterday. I can hear the women in the adjoining cell talking about it still. In this cell we have tired of it for the moment and are thinking our own thoughts. Erica is writing a statement of her position. She is still for serving out sentences—with people breaking their fasts as they have to. I have written one, too—taking the same stand but urging, if an earlier date is to be set, then the earliest possible: tomorrow—and Yvonne has signed her name to this. Edie is for leaving. She thinks the project was perhaps doomed from the start because it was "a little bit vainglorious"; we should admit the realities of the situation now.

I can hear Michele talking next door: "It hurts to see the difference in Brad." He had become so wonderfully human on the Walk, she recalls; now that's been starved out of him; see how rigid he is.

In the distance a prisoner is crying, "Oh God oh God oh God!" He has apparently been handcuffed to the bars, because he cries, "The city wants to tear my hands off! Oh, they hurt so! Oh, I hope they're paralyzed!"

The woman in the lower bunk tosses restlessly.

Now Michele is talking about how it will split the group to have some people get out at one time, some at another, some at still another. She is saying that she has seen the hurt in us all, and now we are being split from each other, too, and we should all of us get out as fast as possible and be a family again—start the work of healing again before the healing gets too hard.

Erica has been listening too and suddenly speaks up: "Look, Michele! I grant you it would be much messier than if we all got out in one group, but we've never acted as a close-order drill!"

We haven't, by any means. Each person in the group has felt very free, within limits, to make his protest in his own way—according to his sense of his own strength and according to his sense of what will be most effective. This has always seemed to me by far the best policy, for it made it both more likely that each of us would be able to follow through with an action taken, and more likely that we would become real, as individuals, to those we confronted. For a while it might confuse them—as one of us chose to walk, another to go limp, another to walk part of the way only—but it would also make them realize more quickly that we were not just following orders but acting out of conscience. It is obvious at this moment, too, however, how thoroughly it can complicate our lives. Because we have acted as individuals, we are being punished accordingly, and the thing that makes it hardest at this point to advocate serving out sentences is the thought that it asks much more of some people than of others. The burden is great on those who have refused to walk to court and so haven't even been sentenced yet. It is a good guess that whether or not they ever are tried, the city will release them with relief when the last of the rest of us get out; but no one can be absolutely sure of this. I begin to brood on the irony that those who have taken the boldest initial stand now make others feel—and feel themselves, most of them—that we should give up the idea of persisting as long as we might.

I begin to waver in my own self. The thought of the men who would have to stick it out in the hole weighs on me heavily too. I remember again Brad urging all of them to steel themselves. With part of my mind I am hoping against hope that they will decide to, after all, and that the statements some of us are writing will make a difference to them; but even as I hope so, I ask myself whether it is right, after they have hesitated, to put any kind of pressure on them at all. Men are conscripted for battles of another kind, and then expected to act simply upon command—so that, as Simone Weil points out, war involves a government first of all in violence against its own citizens. But to force anyone into nonviolent struggle would be a contradiction in terms.

Yvonne is arguing with Michele now: "We can't overprotect their psyches." There's a difference between love and sentimentality, she is saying. Michele seems to be assuming that it would be better for them if we gave up at this point; but it might be worse for them, after all—if as a group we abandoned the political and moral perceptions we know are valid.

I agree with her. But still I feel uneasy. How can we make sure that we are not bullying one another?

Erica is making the point: "It's coercing *other* people, of course, if we set a terminal date."

Perhaps some should stay in and some should pay their fines and get out. But this would be no solution, either. The "hurt" Michele has seen in the men is more than physical. If most of them bailed out and most of the

[139

women stayed in, it would hardly be healing. I think of the tortured note Gene Keyes sent to us when he decided to walk to court, after first planning to refuse. Sometime in March he is due to be picked up as a C. O. and probably jailed for a long term, so he needs time between jail sentences to set his affairs in order, and he didn't want to risk an indefinite sentence here. He might have assumed that we would find this easy to understand, but his note ran: "After endless agonized mulling, I am beginning to think of signing a walk-to-court . . . It's taken a long long time for me to explain this to myself, so think of my problem explaining it to you, since above all I don't want to break ranks with Kit, Michele, Candy, and Mary and the rest . . ." I think of Allen Cooper, who decided to go on a water fast like Ray's. After three trips to the hospital to be force-fed, he found it impossible to keep it up and he paid his fine and bailed out. (Bill Supernaw has done the same: "I bit off more than I could chew.") Allen was at the meeting yesterday, and in the midst of the discussion of what we should all decide to do, he went into a long explanation to us of how he hadn't broken the fast while he was still in jail, only once he had gotten out, and of how he had decided at a certain point that he could be a greater help to us on the outside—obviously tortured by the thought that we might no longer count him as one of us. When I hugged him at the end of the meeting his face showed such astonishment and relief that I was startled. I think of a note from Tyrone, who broke his fast some days ago; I think of a note we received from Peter Gregonis—titled: "Report on Us Weaklings."

We may continually emphasize individual choice, but the pressure everybody feels not to "break ranks" is still acute. Our loyalty to one another makes it inevitable; pride makes it inevitable too; and clearly the pressure is especially painful for the men. The fact that, except for myself, the women on the project have extraordinary stamina hasn't made it easier for them. Ralph has written, "Hi dear ladies, most powerful of creatures . . . Now I can truly admire the female more than the male—and that's the way it should be anyway." But Ralph is not one of those who has "broken" and, plainly, those who have cannot take his words for comfort. Gene in one of his letters to the women has spoken of their strength and thanked them for their notes "which are just too joyful to be so, darn it, darn it!" His muted cry—"darn it, darn it!"—disturbs my thoughts again. Is Michele right and *is* it time to get out?

Yvonne is saying to Michele, "I don't like your group-therapy conception of this project." Michele is saying, "I can last till March 5, and I know others can, and the extra time won't kill us, as you say; but I can see the hurt in each of us, and in the men I'm pretty sure it's worse. I want to stop it."

Erica announces that she has finished writing out her statement. Michele says gloomily, "It sounds as if you're going to read it. I'm braced."

The drunken woman on the lower bunk sits up suddenly and exclaims, "Oh, I wanna go home!"

TWELVE

A. J. and Dave have appeared at last—not to call us to a second meeting, but to give us news. A. J. spoke hurriedly in whispers to the women next door; Dave spoke with us—first scanning our faces with a look that combined anxiety and new hope.

It seems that, after our meeting, C. B. gave the Albany Movement a report of our situation, and Marion Page, the Movement's secretary, came to the Walk's head-quarters and declared, "Your people in jail have done it —they've started up the Albany Movement again. We can't stand by now and not support them, because if they're defeated it's a defeat for us again." Old as he is, and in ill health, he has committed himself, for one, to go to jail if necessary. The Movement is planning something for Saturday, a week from today, involving voter registration. Dave told us, "I'm afraid it's not going to be anything very big," but he and A. J. are recommending to all the group that we hang on at least this extra week to see what comes of it.

So there is hope again. I caution myself not to hope too much.

They brought some other news. In response to a letter from Brad, two Quakers from the Friends Service Committee have arrived in town to see whether they can be of help as mediators between us and the city's white power structure. And of course A. J. and Dave too will keep seeking interviews. Dave searched our faces again before he left. "If you think you can hang on . . ." He urged that no one in the group keep on fasting who feels that he or she has gone far enough.

Edie and Yvonne are discussing now how many people are likely to persist in the fast and how many are likely to break it. They both feel sure they can persist—though Yvonne feels awful today; she says, "I'm almost looking forward to the next force-feeding." Edie is astonished at how well *she* continues to feel; she doesn't really understand it. She says, "I have a sense that my body can just go on and on." I don't understand it, either, for she was one of the thinnest among us to begin with, and she is by now all bone. Her shoulder blades stick through her cotton shirt like chicken wings. Her nose stands out of her face with an almost severe prominence—her cheeks have fallen so—and her whole face looks longer now than it used to. I stare at her, for she reminds me suddenly of some dramatic figure I cannot quite place. Is it one of Chagall's etchings of a gaunt Old Testament patriarch? Or is it a figure from a Kabuki drama I watched once—a dying prince? Above her wasted face, the thick puff of her glossy purply-black hair looks now almost like a Japanese wig. But her glance belies the likeness; it is humorous still. She takes out the pack of cards. "Madame Zoroastra will tell all your fortunes."

TEN P.M.

We have had another visitor for a few hours—a poor woman from out of town who had been drinking for three days and wanted to stop; she went to the local hospital to ask for help but was turned away, so then she came here and asked to be locked up until a bus was due to leave for her home town. Here they took her in. She has been sick to her stomach and then has stretched out on the lower bunk where I now lie, and it still reeks of her breath.

I try not to think about it and I recall to myself C. B.'s visit toward the end of the day. He took off his hat and set it up on the flat steel roof above our heads, took off his jacket and folded it and stuck it up there, then faced us with an air, for him, almost lighthearted—clearly very pleased about what has just happened. He whispered, "They've finally seen that we are welded together by the fact that we both need our civil liberties." He has never before told us that he thinks we *are* bound together. He stayed even longer than usual, and he and Edie joked together, matching wits with more than their usual spirit.

Yvonne is sighing in her sleep; the sounds seem wrenched from her. Edie puts down the book she is reading and listens. Then we both sit up in bed, for there is a commotion outside, a cop is cursing, somebody is being dragged. Yvonne and Erica sit up too, all of us awake suddenly, for the new prisoner has just cried out, "Greetings to you, peacewalkers!"

We call back, "Who are you?"

"John——"

"John who?"

He spells it out for us: Papworth.

"Where are you from?"

His diction is clear and crisp: "London."

We wake more completely.

"I bring you greetings from the Committee of 100!"

We stare at one another. We call, "Were you at Mercer Avenue?" (Our headquarters.)

"Yes. They're mustering support for you; all the wires are humming!" He relates for us cheerily, "I told them here at the jail that I thought you had all been wrongfully imprisoned and I was here to ask for your immediate release. I said I wouldn't leave until you were all allowed to leave with me. So here we all are, you might say. Your Chief Pritchett wasn't a bit glad to see me. In fact, he threw me quite forcibly against a door. My face is a bit bruised. Not badly, of course." He inquires about *our* health.

I lie back on my bunk, lightheaded. No, the Chief cannot be very happy now. On the eve of his vacation, everything has been shaken up again. It appears that our strength has *not* been expended. Here we still are, in spite of his recent hopes; and we are even being reinforced. From London! I think dizzily: How close, how close we came to bailing out—because no sign of reinforcements was visible to us; neither John nor the Albany Movement had given us an advance sign. How often we have to remind ourselves that in a struggle like this the support our actions gain can remain invisible until the very moment that it is given.

Mary Suzuki is calling, "What do you look like, John?"

He answers, "I'm forty-two, five foot ten, hazel eyes . . ." He asks, "What are all your names? Shout them, because they've taken away my hearing aid."

MONDAY, FEBRUARY 17 (22ND DAY)
AFTERNOON

There is new reason to hope, and yet I am finding it harder than before to live through the hours. On other days I have suffered from discouragement or fear, and on every day from discomfort, but today for the first time I feel unutterably tired of being in here, and this is harder to bear.

I woke this morning and stared at the ceiling formed by the other bunk, close above me; woke, but felt that some part of me had still to waken; lay there waiting for this to happen, but just as the walls of our cage hold us, so the walls of my own being seemed to hold trapped and inert some formerly active part of me. I climbed out of my bunk, splashed water in my face at the sink, and then tried standing up for a while in the small floor space, but then lay down again—still locked dismally within my own fatigue. For the first time I truly know how it feels to want to rattle the bars. The bars, the steel walls, for the first time impress me as inexorably what they are.

A cockroach is wandering along the wall beside my bunk. A creature able to come and go! I watch him with desperate attention, trying to free my own spirit by following with my eyes his energetic course. His meanderings bring him to the front of the cage, and he begins to walk lightly along one of the horizontal bars. With the window behind him, his delicate hairy legs are outlined with light and his translucent body shines like a piece of amber. I watch him for a long time, finding comfort in it.

I hear Yvonne and Edie talking together. Yvonne is saying, "I begin to feel as though I'm sliding down a toboggan." In the past few days things have of course become harder still for most of my friends. Yvonne has started again to have to be careful each time she stands up—not to black out. Even Erica is beginning to feel the fast now; she has strange sensations in her ears as though she had water in them. And Saturday Michele reported having trouble urinating. Erica wrote a worried note out about this, and a Quaker doctor, Arthur Evans, who is here from Denver to be of what help he can, tried again for permission to get in to see us, but again he was denied —"We can't let every Tom, Dick and Harry in to see them!" Michele is angry at Erica now because of the extra fuss that has been made, and she says she is really all right. When A. J. came at noon yesterday he questioned her carefully, talked with the rest of us for the few minutes allowed him, took Edie's hand and then burst out, "Oh I want to get you all out of here so much!"

He had nothing very new to report. He had told Pritchett, before he left for Nassau, that all bets were off now about terminal dates—as the Albany Movement was planning demonstrations for the twenty-second and we would naturally want to show our solidarity with them. The Chief managed to keep an impassive face. A. J. has sent a wire to the Department of Justice, asking that they investigate the lack of civil liberties here and issue a public report. He and Dave have an appointment to see City Manager Roos and Mayor Davis.

After A. J.'s visit, Edie began to feel very strange. She took her pulse, which is normally between 100 and 108, and it was 55. When C. B. came at the end of the day she was feeling so weak that she didn't even sit up; she just stretched out a limp hand to him, and he stared at her, alarmed. Last night she talked strangely in her sleep. She was awake through most of the night, however; she lies there now, she says, and feels sleep climbing her body, but when it reaches her head, it stops. Today she hasn't moved from her bunk, and so a little while ago I brought her a damp washcloth and washed her face, her hands, her feet for her. She is beginning not to know herself, she told me, and she is going to break her fast, because she doesn't want to reach a state where she would want to bail out.

Yes, one begins to be a stranger to oneself; this is the most difficult feeling of all one has to struggle with in here. Even I, who am merely on a token fast, know it a little. In the middle of the night last night, I was sitting on the toilet and I leaned my elbow on the sink beside me, wearily, and leaned my cheek on my hand—and my face didn't feel to my hand like my own face. A sensation of utter desolation startled me. I felt: Am I sure it is I?

[147

How much of me can waste away and my self remain? The day of the meeting I felt a similar shock when Dave and I hugged. When I have hugged people before, there has always been some sort of pillowing of flesh between us, but this day I felt my ribs knock against Dave's ribs. I felt: Is there no more to me than this?

LATER

We have heard from Tony that he plans to break his fast today; and Mary has had a note from Michael, reporting from the hole that Barry and Alan have broken theirs. He added, "I have reached that stage where one starts to feel sorry for oneself . . . Write me a letter . . . Your self-pitying friend . . ." And we have had a note from Ray:

"From one Cool Kat to a group of Cool Kittens—Hello Dolls, Well for some of us this is our 22d day in this wonderful jail. Reservation by none other than Chief himself Pritchett. Hey I just read he's now vacationing in Florida. While we're vacationing in his great hotel, where we have bars in every room . . . Do you girls realize this is our 22d day here. And we all are still loving these people . . . I had a dream (ah hell) that one day Pritchett said, 'Okay you Pacifists, go ahead and walk anywhere your hearts tell you.' This was not a dream, this was a daydream! . . . So like laterville and gonesville. Raysville. P.S.: These words come from a lameville, trying to be hip."

We hear a cop walking back into the larger cell block. John calls to him from his cell behind ours, "Aren't we ever allowed any exercise?"

"No," the cop tells him.

"Doesn't the Geneva Convention say a prisoner is to be given some exercise?"

148]

"You don't run this jail, John," the cop informs him.
John replies cheerily, "I declare!"
Now he calls, "What did you say, loves?"
We call back, "It wasn't we."
Another prisoner wants to engage him in conversation:
"What have they got you in for?"
"Loitering, as it happens," John answers.
"When you get out, let's go loitering together."
"I don't really think you'd care to go loitering the way
I do."
"Don't you like puss, Englishman?"
"What?" asks John.
The other man laughs wildly. "Don't you like pussy?"
"I don't understand," John calls back.
The other yells, "It's kind of late to be explaining the
facts of life to you!"
I look across at Edie. A few days ago she would have
laughed at this, but she is just lying there, looking at the
ceiling.

STILL LATER

Clarence, the run-around, with a timid smile, appears at
the bars with a large brown paper bag of food for Edie.
She has sent a note out to headquarters asking to have a
few special things bought for her, because the prison food
is harsh fare on which to break a fast. She sits up with
a start and holds out her arms for the bag; then, hugging
it to her, seating herself crosslegged, opens it and peers in
as though afraid to find it empty. She rapidly inspects
the contents and her eyes brighten: bananas, apples, a jar
of honey, cottage cheese, crackers, some tiny marshmallows. She peels a banana—slowly. She is about to take
a bite when she stops, unscrews the top of the honey jar,
dips the banana into it, and then puts it into her mouth.

[149

We all watch, hypnotized, as she begins to eat it—she is so entirely concentrated upon the act, like someone receiving the sacrament. It is Life itself she eats.

In the distance we hear a strange small cry of joy. Tony has just received *his* bag of special foods.

Yvonne has been reading poetry aloud lately, at my request; a friend has sent in an anthology. Now I hand her the volume and she leafs through it and begins to read one of Donne's sonnets:

> *"At the round earth's imagin'd corners, blow*
> *Your trumpets, Angells, and arise, arise*
> *From death, you numberlesse infinities*
> *Of soules, and to your scattered bodies goe . . ."*

As she reads, I feel the terrible weariness that has held me cramped within myself crack like a shell; I stare at the walls and they no longer look solid but fragile as shell too, easily burst; the bars look widely spaced; our cells seems airy. A cockroach runs across my foot and out into the corridor and then back into the cell and then out again. Edie spreads some cottage cheese on a cracker.

TUESDAY, FEBRUARY 18 (23D DAY)
MORNING

I wake and look across at Edie lying on the bunk across from me. She is sleeping soundly, her cheeks flushed with new color, her lips rosy again too and curled in a new smile. A few days ago someone sent some nail polish to our cell and she and Yvonne both did their nails. Her hands are flung up near her cheeks now and the nails gleam, pearly. She looks like some maiden in a myth, just born from the sea, still asleep on the shore. As I stare at her she wakes, takes her pulse, then utters a little cry. It is almost normal again.

The doctor has paid his morning visit. He told Yvonne, "You'd better begin to eat, too, you know. The Chief is in Nassau."

"What has that to do with it?" Yvonne asked him.

He stood there for a minute, then could only answer, "Well, he's in Nassau."

Does this mean that no one will be taken to the hospital while the Chief is away, because he is the only one who can give the order? I struggle with the fear that it is so.

Sergeant Hamilton has just dropped by for a moment, too: "Do you all feel you could run a foot race this morning?"

In the cell behind us John begins to recite aloud from Shaw's *Back to Methuselah*. He has the elocution of a Shakespearean actor. Yvonne puts down the blue sweater she is knitting, to listen. I study her. This is her twenty-seventh day. Her smile, once almost constant, has at last wasted from her face; the corners of her mouth are now downturned. Her cheeks are deeply shadowed; the high cheekbones jut forth like polished stone; her upper lip, strangely puffy, is drawn back from her teeth. She looks like a brooding lioness.

A note arrives from Barry, describing the special diets on which he and Marv and Alan broke their fasts— "Powdered milk, pablum, honey, raisins . . . Never has anything tasted so good! . . . Ecstasy!"—and then giving us a report about the others: "Ralph was made for fasting. On his twenty-third day he is just beginning to lose steam. To my amazement John-i-thin seems all right

[151

. . . I figured he would need medical attention in a week . . . Ken suffers quietly . . . Gene could have serious trouble any time. He doesn't call a fast a fast unless it's liberty or death. I don't know which is closer for him. He doesn't move much at all any more."

It is noon—the hour when they allow A. J. to visit, and we begin to listen for his light step. There it is, and we all move up closer to the bars. Good news is written on his face; behind his glasses his eyes dance with the queer intense light which I have often seen translate him from a frail old man into one without age.

He speaks in whispers again, very slowly and carefully, so that it will all be clear to us. First, the mayor and the city manager have now said that they won't make any proposals themselves but would be open to receiving a new proposal from us. In the meantime the two Quakers who have come down to try to help us, James Bristol and Cal Geiger, have been having talks with local ministers— after being refused interviews with a number of city officials—and they have been joined by another Friends Service Committee man, Carl Zeitlow, who happened to be in Albany. Yesterday these three met with a Presbyterian minister, the head of the Ministerial Association—and their talks "started something." Reverend X.* had been defending the position taken by the city, arguing that Oglethorpe Avenue was a perfectly reasonable route to have assigned us. Bristol asked whether he was aware that the city strictly specified that we must walk up the south

* Reverend X. does not object to my identifying him as the head of the local ministerial association, but he has asked me not to use his name in these pages—because he still does not really approve of us.

152]

side of that avenue, couldn't even walk up the north side —obviously because it bordered the white section of town. Reverend X. hadn't realized this and looked a little troubled, and when Bristol then asked whether he thought the city might allow us at least to walk up the north side, he answered that he couldn't say, but he felt that it was possible. Carl Zeitlow suddenly thought of another compromise: what if the Walk divided, with some of us walking up Oglethorpe but some of us going through the downtown shopping area? Then they could say that we had walked where *they* wanted and we could say that we had walked where *we* wanted. At this point Mr. X. suggested a second meeting later in the day, to which he would invite three other ministers—another Presbyterian, a Methodist and a Baptist—and this meeting A. J. and Dave had attended. But before it took place Reverend X. had a further thought and made a telephone call, which he reported to all of them: it struck him that the city had once decided that six people constitute a parade, and so he called City Manager Roos, who happens to be a fellow Presbyterian with whom he is congenial, and sounded him out as to whether *five* of us might not be permitted to enter briefly the downtown shopping area and then rejoin the rest of us—on the north side of Oglethorpe.

A. J. now grasps the bars between us. Roos didn't actually say so, but he virtually told Mr. X. that if the walkers would accept that compromise it could be worked out with the city. So A. J. is asking for our approval. We should know that when he reported all this to C. B. and Slater King, to Marion Page and to Phil Davis of S.N.C.C., every one of them felt it would be a distinct victory, much more of a victory than any of them had dreamed was possible. If we approve, the four ministers are willing to act as our mediators. We all nod our heads

[153

mutely, then whisper, "Yes, we approve." Edie manages to kiss A. J. through the bars. He hurries off. We sit for a moment in dazed silence and then Yvonne asks, "If any of you believe in prayer, will you please pray?"

THIRTEEN

WE ARE still waiting for further news. It is time for C. B.'s visit, and perhaps he will bring it. I have tried to make the afternoon pass more quickly and, by a kind of magic, to make the news be good, by finishing the job I have been working at intermittently—scratching high on the wall above the sink some lines from Blake:

Bring me my Bow of burning gold:
Bring me my Arrows of desire:
Bring me my Spear: O clouds unfold!
Bring me my Chariot of fire.

I will not cease from Mental Fight,
Nor shall my Sword sleep in my hand
Till we have built Jerusalem
In England's green and pleasant Land.

I have used the metal tip of a Scripto pencil for scratching, and a little while ago I put the final period. Now I am exhausted.

Earlier this afternoon Mary's friend Peter Light arrived in jail. Apparently A. J. tried to discourage him from coming in at just this moment, but Peter had finally decided that he must join us—and did. About two-thirty we heard the familiar sound of a body being dragged and then Peter's voice calling out to us. He had tried passing out leaflets at the front steps about conditions in

[155

here and managed to get rid of two. He called out to Mary Suzuki in a tremulous voice, "Mary, I'm noncooperating quite a bit!"

Now Mary is calling to him (they have put him in a cell just behind us, next to John's): "Peter, I miss you!"

He calls, "What did you say?"

She calls again, "I miss you!"

He asks, "What?"

Half laughing, half irritated, she calls more loudly, "I said I miss you!"

"Oh!" he exclaims. "Oh, I miss *you!*"

A distant prisoner calls to John, "Hey, limey, was there such a person as Robin Hood?"

There is the knock on the wall which we have been waiting for. It is not C. B.—who has been detained—but Attorney Jackson. His smile seems to me one of extraordinary sweetness; he suddenly reminds me of a smiling angel in a Renaissance painting. He is whispering, "The proposal seems to be acceptable." Without reason, I feel a sharp pain in my stomach. He whispers, "Better keep it confidential still, but if it does go through, you should all be out of here the day after tomorrow."

We all embrace as in a trance.

LATER

A cop brings in a new prisoner, locks him in the cell with John and walks off. We hear the man ask abruptly, "Are you a freedom walker like he said?"

We all sit up. We cannot hear John's reply.

"You better make your peace with God!" the man is yelling. "So you like niggers?"

We strain to hear what John is saying but still cannot make it out; and then we hear the sound of blows.

156]

Yvonne presses close to the door and calls out, "Can someone come? A man is being beaten up in here!"

Kit speaks up from the next cell: "Don't, Yvonne! When we're outside, we never ask the police for protection!" Michele agrees.

Yvonne tells them, "Sometimes I can't take smugness!" But she doesn't call again.

The noise in the cell behind us stops.

Mary calls, "Peter, what happened?"

Peter answers softly, "It was John."

"Is he all right?"

Now John answers for himself—even more softly, "Yes."

WEDNESDAY, FEBRUARY 19 (24TH DAY)
EVENING

We are still waiting for definitive news. A. J. came at noon and showed us the letter we are sending to the authorities, making the new proposal, and told us that it might be evening before we would have final word. His mood was high; but when C. B. visited at about five o'clock he reported that the letter was at that point being shown to the city commissioners—and most of us stopped believing that the proposal would be accepted. Haven't we been told often enough that the commissioners are solidly against us? We had somehow understood that Roos and the mayor had decided they could act without them.

In the distance, Peter Gregonis suddenly calls to Tyrone, "Tomorrow's the day, man!"

Yvonne calls out to him, "Peter, just cut it out, will you?"

It is hard to look at Yvonne today—she is so sick. The doctor has told her again that she had better start to eat—

[157

"You've proved something to yourself by now; you've made the record for the group; twenty-eight days for you; that's enough"—and Kit reports overhearing him telling Pritchett's secretary as he was leaving, "She's carrying it too far!" It seems more and more clear that he is not going to take her to the hospital again on his own initiative.

This afternoon she tried to wash her hair, just in case we should really be getting out. But when she began to try to rinse it, using the bottle in which Pritchett once brought me orange juice, she spilled the water all over herself, unable to judge distances properly any longer. Edie washed her hair for her.

Assistant Chief Friend dropped by for a visit and reported that Pritchett had telephoned from Nassau. "He's worried about you all," he said. "The Chief's very human, you know." We told him that we knew. "I mean, he's very kind." As a matter of fact, we have discovered that we miss the Chief—we seem to have grown fond of him. But we are not sure just how kind he intends to be to us, and we are wondering what voice he is having in these deliberations now.

There is the sound of a cell door slamming, and then the voice of an old man who has been in here before: "Well, God bless every one of you!"—the words hopelessly slurred.

"You can't stay out three days, can you?" someone asks.

"I'm an old man," he says. "I want to drink a little first and then I'm going to bed."

Edie is sitting on a top bunk lighting a series of matches and with elaborate care toasting over their brief flames some of the tiny marshmallows that came in her package of food. Erica is sitting on the other top bunk, her legs swung over the edge, calmly answering letters. Can she really be calm? Yvonne is stretched out on the bunk across from mine, staring at nothing, her mouth slack. Suddenly she sits up, crying, "Edie, for God's sake, do you have to toast those things? The smell of them is going to finish me off!"

Someone calls, "John, John, shake that man and stop his snoring!"

It brings me abruptly back to myself. All day my mind has been wandering. I begin to imagine myself home; then suddenly I wake with a start to the fact that I am still here and waiting, and I ask myself what time of day it is, having no idea at all. And then I look across at Yvonne. I ask myself, in agitation: If we are *not* released tomorrow? And then my mind jumps somewhere else again, and then I wake with a start.

Peter Light is calling, "My cellmate's fallen off his bed and been sick all over the floor. I wish to God they'd clean it up."

A prisoner in another cell calls, "They will—next week."

THURSDAY, FEBRUARY 20 (25TH DAY)
NOON

It is A. J. at last. His face looks pinched and gray. He tells us very softly: there is no definite word yet, but Reverend X. has called Stephen Roos and Roos sounds very much less sure of himself now. Mr. X. says Roos also brought up the possibility that one of us might do something unexpected—might, for instance, suddenly go limp on the street—though he did also express confidence in A. J. and his word, once given.

A. J. begins to gesture emphatically as he whispers,

[159

"There is a terrific power struggle going on. And people outside are sending in more and more telegrams now—prominent people, too: Norman Thomas, Norman Cousins, Congressmen Ryan and Lindsay. We have also checked to see what names we could find of liberal Northerners on the board of directors of business corporations which have local branches here, and we let some of these men know what is happening; it's just possible that at least some of them will bring pressure to bear. Meanwhile, we have been in touch with London, and the British consul has put through a telephone call to the authorities here, questioning them about John's imprisonment and beating. His situation has been mentioned on the floor of Parliament. It's possible that our State Department has been calling Albany, because supporters in Montreal have protested to the Department about the violation to Mary's and Michael's and Peter's civil liberties; and, by the way, *their* situation has been mentioned on the floor of the Canadian Parliament. It's certain that the Department of Justice has been making inquiries. And even one Southerner has raised his voice: a long letter has appeared in the Atlanta *Constitution* objecting to the treatment we have received . . ."

Yvonne is not feeling well enough to sit up for A. J.'s visit, and he keeps glancing at her as he speaks, his face flinching slightly each time. Just about to leave, he reaches out and lightly strokes her hair.

LATER

I asked Sergeant Cress, when he brought us clean mattress covers earlier today, whether he would let me go into the next cell to help those people change theirs, as they were weak from fasting, and he agreed and left both doors unlocked for a while, so we were all able to visit,

160]

and also to stretch our legs. Yvonne found that she couldn't walk, however, and just sat down in the corridor. Erica is still the most energetic among us and did most of the work, though she is very tired now. Before we returned to our own cells I told Cress, "I thank you with all my heart," and he answered gravely, to my surprise, "I think you mean that."

Mary Suzuki is thin as cardboard, and she coughs all the time. Kit's eyes have dulled, and Candy is a little hard to communicate with; withdrawn into herself, she apparently sleeps most of the time now. But Michele's face especially haunts me—haggard as though she were staring at death, her yellow hair plastered to the side of her head strangely, as though she had just been pulled up from the bottom of a well.

She and Yvonne have begun to discuss again what we had better do if the compromise agreement falls through and if nothing develops out of the Albany Movement's plans for Saturday the twenty-second. Michele is still for getting out; Yvonne is still for serving our sentences—or for waiting at least until March 5. "I'm really just recommending that we finish what we started." She speaks, too, of the political pressures that are obviously building up.

Michele is saying, "I'm not interested in political pressures."

"Then you're not being responsible," Yvonne tells her.

Michele begins to speak again about the hurt that is being done to some people—and not just a physical hurt.

Yvonne asks, "What if the situation demands it? This is the real world."

Michele asserts doggedly, "I think our stopping would actually have a more real effect. Wasn't it the fact that we were giving up that made the Albany Movement decide to act? I have more faith in a clear and open and honest humble-proud defeat and the effect this could have to inspire people than in some little bit of advance under special circumstances." And she just states simply, "It doesn't feel natural to stay in jail any longer."

My feelings are strangely rent as I listen to them, for it is Yvonne who seems to me to be talking sense, and I am hoping with all my strength that her view will prevail among us, and yet in this exchange it is Michele who is most intensely real for me. She has one truth to declare: People don't belong in jail. Certain other truths, at the moment, are outside the field of her vision. She is too starved, I think, to be able to look at them all. (She suddenly exclaims to Yvonne, "I know that I probably shouldn't have come into jail this second time!") But her vision of that one truth is sharp. Her whole being is now concentrated upon it; she stares at it like a seer: we don't belong here, no one belongs here. She not only sees it, she is the figure of it—her very flesh speaks it. There are some lines from Blake on the walls of that cell too; I scratched them up before four of us were moved into a second cell:

> A robin red breast in a cage
> Puts all heaven in a rage!

Michele's very person now seems to me scratched with the truth of these lines. So that even while I want to say to her, There is so much that you are forgetting, I want to exclaim, You are right! Yes, she is like some distracted figure out of the ancient Greek theater, a wild woman crying out her one truth—which she can indeed see.

As they sit there arguing, I hear one prisoner calling to another in the distance, "The fuzz wanted me to change my mattress cover, so I got in it and zipped it up, the motherfucker!" He is answered by wild laughter. Then I hear a cop going back there, and suddenly we hear a gasping cry and we all sit still; one of the prisoners

162]

cries out, "Oh! My mother is dead!" and bursts into desperate sobs. We hear the cop who has brought him the news walking away. The prisoner in the cell with John cries, "What a place to hear it!" and for a long time the men and women in all the cells are silent, listening to the weeping man.

We still wait for some definitive word. The clock across the street has struck noon, struck the quarter hour and half past, but A. J. has not appeared. I lie on a lower bunk and for the hundredth time read the scratchings on the wall: LINDA HASTY AND DAVID HUGGINS. JIMMY LEEP. SHIRLEY HALE SLEPT HERE WITHOUT HUEGH PEAVY BUT HE WAS CLOSE I LOVE HIM. THE MELTON BROTERS WAS HERE.

I pick up a note that has come from Ray and reread it: ". . . Girls, I have started eating candy again. No food, just candy. I thought I would tell youse. I'm sorry but that's the way it is. I guess and know youse are stronger than I am . . ."

How many people does that leave still fasting? I try to figure it up. Six women. Among the men: Brad, Ken, Ralph, Gene, John-i-thin. Peter Light—who has just begun, of course. John Papworth has written us that he's unable to fast.

I turn over on my side. It is becoming hard to find any position in which it is comfortable to lie. All my bones seem to rub against each other. My buttocks are very sore, and my hips, my shoulders. I decide to climb up to the top bunk, where Yvonne sits cross-legged, knitting the last rows of her blue sweater. She holds it up for me to see: "Anyway, I'll have made this." F cheeks are quite

[163

drained of color, and the skin around her eyes is darkened as though it were bruised. This morning Dr. Hilsman asked her still again, "Just how long do you intend to go?" When she told him that her sentence is up a week from tomorrow, he said, "I don't think you had better go that long." I keep hearing that phrase in my head now.

I look at my watch. It says twelve-fifty. Is A. J. really not coming? I ask Yvonne, "What does your watch say?" The muscles of her face jerk in the imitation of a smile. She answers, "Tic toc."

That is A. J.'s step. He seems almost to be stumbling as he approaches us; just before he reaches our cage he looks down at his feet as though uncertain of the ground. We all press close to the bars, and for a long moment he just looks at us. He hardly needs to speak after that look. I seem to hear his words spoken in slow motion:

"We received a letter from Roos yesterday afternoon—turning the proposal down on the grounds that it would pose too many traffic problems. The ministers were shocked at this reply and they are now angry too, because when they questioned it they were virtually told to hold their tongues. So they have learned something about this city—seen that what they think about its problems is considered irrelevant. Actually, of course, they learned this once before, back in 1961 during the demonstrations King led. One of them said yesterday, 'We really got the message then.' But I don't think they ever quite faced up to it. This is the first time they have said aloud to each other: 'We are considered irrelevant here.' " There is the smallest spark of expectation in his eye as he tells us this, but then I see it dim. "Dave and I have just had a meeting with them, and they are now holding a meeting of their own. They are composing a new proposal—though they have no real hope for it. This proposal is that five of you

164]

start out alone and walk into the downtown shopping area, then return to headquarters; *then* the entire Walk would set forth and walk out of town along Oglethorpe . . ."

Edie takes out the pack of cards. "I don't want to hear any fortunes," Yvonne tells her sharply. "A game of rummy?" Edie asks. But Yvonne decides to try to take a nap—she's feeling nauseated—and she climbs down to the bunk I have left vacant. I glance down at her and she lies flattened out as though all her strength has been taken. Her cheeks are now as collapsed as those of an old woman without teeth; her nose has an exaggeratedly pinched look as though she smelled something very bad; her mouth is open; her hands grasp her stomach. She looks like death. I glance across at Edie. She is staring at Yvonne, too, and I see tears in her eyes.

A cop walks through the alley, whistling. On a pipe against the brick wall across from us, the sparrow I have noticed before sits and turns its head from left to right, flits up into the air and then alights again. A sweet clear afternoon light is flooding the alley, and the brick wall behind the fluttering bird shimmers before my eyes like water.

A prisoner who was calling to John Papworth a little while ago begins to call to Peter Light. John and Peter have been moved into the same cell. "Are you working for the peace movement too? That's a hell of an occupation! Peace be with you! How about that?"

Peter starts to answer and the man suddenly inquires, "Have you been dicking that half-Japanese girl?"

There is an abrupt pause; then Peter tells him, "I don't think I'm going to answer you."

The man calls, "I'm fixing to get out and I may go by

[165

and give her a little bit. Oh ho oh ho!" Then: "Ask her if she'll give me a little bit."

Peter says firmly, "Say that once more and I'll not speak to you again."

"Is she a nigger?" the man calls.

Peter controls his voice and asks, "What's your name?"

"Charlie."

"Charlie," Peter explains carefully, "unless you can be decent and have some consideration for other people's feelings, you can't expect to hold conversations with them."

Charlie informs him, "Someone may lynch you, you know!" Then he resumes his questions about Mary Suzuki. Peter no longer replies. Charlie at last lapses into silence too. Then he suddenly rattles the bars violently. He shouts, "I say there, bloke, how are you?"

Peter doesn't answer.

So he calls, "Hey, limey, somebody's fucking with your girl over there!"

Erica asks, "Why has he such a hang-up?"

Michele from the next cell declares with passion, "People who stay in here too long get desperate!"

"Take it easy," Erica tells her.

Charlie calls, "Hey, blook!" Then in a voice infinitely plaintive, "Hey, John the bloke, hey, Peter the blook!"

Nobody answers him.

In the distance Peter Gregonis begins to sigh upon his harmonica the tune of *Michael, Row the Boat Ashore.*

I look down at Yvonne, look again. Is she asleep or unconscious? To my relief, she stirs.

LATE AFTERNOON

There is a knock on the wall. C. B. and "Jack"—Attorney Jackson—have both come to see us. They have no further

166]

word to report. C. B. opens his briefcase and takes out some cigarettes he has bought at Edie's request; then he shuts it again. We hold out our hands for mail, but he tells us, "Your people at Mercer Avenue didn't get the mail to me today."

We stare at him in horror; nobody can speak. We have managed to receive with stoicism the hard news A. J. brought, but this news seems suddenly impossible to bear. C. B. studies us, troubled, then quickly begins a long story to try to divert us. I cannot really concentrate on what he is saying; I just watch his mouth and his hands moving, watch his eyes—drawing some comfort from his presence, and Jack's.

A cop comes down the corridor, taps C. B. on the shoulder: "Reverend Muste is out front and wants to see you."

Jack stays, and I see him searching his brain for some way to cheer us up. He begins to tell us about his last visit to Brad and Ray across the street at the county jail.

C. B. reappears. He is letting Jack finish his sentence, but Edie asks hungrily, "A. J. didn't have our mail, did he?"

C. B. asks, "Would a message from him do in its place?" He gives us a long look, raising his eyebrows, and we look back at him, confused. He begins, then, a long and elaborate sentence—the kind he enjoys spinning out when he and Edie jest. Starting to smile, he brings his sentence to an end: ". . . the ministers' latest proposal has been accepted."

MIDDLE OF THE NIGHT

It is still not clear when we are to be set free. A. J. has asked whether we could not be released tomorrow, considering the agreement that has been reached, and considering the very precarious health of some among us. He

[167

sent his message through C. B., but hasn't yet received an answer. The plan is to let us walk on Monday. Will they want to keep us locked up until that moment? I wince at the thought. Perhaps they are waiting for Pritchett's return tomorrow morning, and he will be the one to decide. Now that the end is near, time crawls; it is hard to believe that the actual moment of our release will ever be reached. For Yvonne, for Michele, for the men in the hole, it must be harder. We live through these hours now as mountain climbers inch up a precipice. I keep dreading that someone will find it impossible to hang on any longer; everybody is so desperately frail. About an hour ago, this nightmare dread with which I am obsessed now seemed to be turning into grotesque reality.

Another drunken woman was led by two cops to our cell, an enormously fat woman this time—blind with drink and with unhappiness, tears running from her eyes, tears and snuff running from the corners of her mouth. I cleared the lower bunk on which I had been lying and asked her whether she didn't want to lie down. She moaned, "Yes," and as I pointed to the empty bed, moved heavily toward it, stooping her tremendous body to enter it. But as I was climbing to Erica's bunk to share it with her, I saw the woman rear up again, like some great bewildered animal, and turn about and move toward the other lower bunk, in which Yvonne lay. She was in a stupor; Yvonne was invisible to her; she began to ease her weight into that space, settling down into it. Yvonne half rose up in bed and thrust out her arms with what remaining strength she had to push the woman from her, and I jumped and threw my arms around her to drag her off. But it was like trying to hold a mountain slide. This was like a scene in some brutally comic short film. I felt a crazy terror, and I caught in Yvonne's eye a wild look which asked the same question: Would there be any breath left in her if the woman did succeed in lying down upon her? We seemed to struggle there forever before the woman herself, becoming dimly conscious that something was wrong, drew off and lurched the step across the cell to the other bunk.

It is two in the morning now; the fat woman is snoring; Yvonne, unable to sleep, has climbed up to talk with Edie, who can't sleep either, and I climb across to join them. We sit in a row, like three cage-weary monkeys, hugging our knees, and joke for a few minutes about the death Yvonne almost suffered; but we are not really joking. The fat woman who has entered our cell looms in the mind of each of us as some terrible symbol of the possibility that we could, even in these last hours, still be destroyed.

A Negro woman in a distant cage who has been crying out earlier in the evening begins to cry again, "Oh help, oh help!" She has a very small baby at home and has begged the cops to let her go to it. She is just in for being drunk. She calls again, "Oh my baby, oh my baby!" She calls, "Officer, officer, help!" But nobody comes. So now she gives a great cry like a fighting cat. She gives another. A male prisoner calls, "Hey, baby," applauding her; another calls, "Beat her ass in!" She begins to utter sharp little cries like the cries of some jungle bird, then longer cries ending in trills. She has apparently decided to try to enjoy herself as best she can. In the cell behind us John wakes and exclaims, "Angels and ministers of grace defend us!" The fat woman wakes.

SATURDAY, FEBRUARY 22 (27TH DAY)
MIDAFTERNOON

We are in this cage still. We were up early and had the few things we have collected in here gathered together—

[169

books, letters, writing materials, toilet articles. I wrapped some of them in the blanket Ray brought in, to make a bundle easy to carry; we had saved the plastic bags in which our mattress covers came, and we packed some of the things into these. And then we waited. We expected to be released after the breakfast hour, if we were to be released today. But that hour came and passed. The morning has passed now, and half the afternoon.

Before breakfast they came and led away the fat woman, to our relief, but no one made any reference at all to our getting out. After breakfast, Dr. Hilsman paid his daily visit, spoke his daily warning to Yvonne about fasting too long—just as though this were a morning like any other. When he had gone, Yvonne exclaimed, "I'm not sure how many false alarms one can live through!" She started to climb up to an upper bunk, and as she reached the top she clutched at her side, grimacing, tears jumping to her eyes.

We expected an early visit from Pritchett—who is back now, and usually drops around at the start of the day— but he didn't appear. At breakfast, though, a post card was delivered to Edie—postmarked Nassau. On one side was a picture of a big Nassau hotel, on the other side the message: "Just passed Cuba. Wish you all were there"— signed by the Chief. This communication delighted us, but added to our sense of living not quite anywhere.

The clock on the tower of the county jail across the street struck nine o'clock, struck its tune for the quarter hour and the half and quarter of. We heard the notes out, each time, in silence. It struck ten, and all its quarter hours; and eleven. Then the Chief came walking down the corridor, calm and smiling. "You don't look very tanned, Chief," Edie told him. When she thanked him for his post card, he blushed slightly and began to tell us about some of the fine people he had met in Nassau. He

170]

had met the island's chief of police, and the chief had introduced him to the governor. He'd never been to Nassau before, but now he wanted to go back. The water was wonderfully blue and clear. We sat waiting, trying to appear calm, and finally he asked, "How many of you are going to feel strong enough to walk on Monday?" He stared hard at Yvonne.

She ventured, "That depends a little on when we get out, Chief. Has the time been set?"

He said, "Well, as soon as all the arrangements have been made. It could be this afternoon." He shrugged— as though to indicate that it might also not be. One point had already been settled, he told us: we would pay a fine to cover the damage to city property for which Ray was responsible. He turned to Edie and asked, "That's fair, isn't it?"

She answered, "I don't know the facts, so I can't judge," and at her lack of enthusiasm he looked almost hurt.

"Do you think you're going to miss us?" Erica asked him. He just stared at her.

After he had gone, Yvonne said, "I don't think it's going to be this afternoon." We have been listening to the clock again. I can neither believe that we won't be released today nor that we will. The hours are unreal. It is difficult to know how to fill them, what to think about or what to let oneself feel.

Sergeant Bass has opened a window for us, and I sit drawing into my lungs the thin current of fresh air. I woke this morning in another of those states in which I find it hard to break entirely out of sleep, all my senses dazed. Even Erica has been dizzy today, and her face has a funny lost look it has never worn before.

I decide to neaten some of the piles of our belongings, so that if they do come for us there will be no delay about

[171

our leaving the cell. I have the irrational feeling that if we delay when that moment arrives, they may just close the door on us again. I climb down from the bunk and fasten the mouths of two of the plastic sacks more securely. And then I line up all our shoes under one bunk—ready to step into. Yvonne looks down at me and smiles and shakes her head. I climb back up to wait again. It is almost three o'clock.

There are steps in the corridor and then we hear the key turning in the lock of the cell next door, hear the door grating open. We scramble off our bunks and stand for a moment in the middle of the floor, rigid. Sergeant Hamilton stands at the door of our cell now, turning the key again; the sound of it echoes and echoes through me, and the sound of the door swinging wide. It takes me a long time to tie my shoe laces; but when I stand up and clutch the bundle I have packed, the door is still wide open.

We file down the corridor and around the corner into the large cell block. Other cops are standing along the way—Assistant Chief Friend, Sergeant Cress, Sergeant Bass—and almost all of them are smiling—smiles that seem half respectful, half puzzled. We shake hands with each of them in turn as we pass. In the large cell block the doors of the men's cells are wide, too, and the men are stepping out of them. We hurry to each other, solemnly kiss each other on the mouth. There is John Papworth, peering into each face. I tell him, "I'm Barbara," and we peer at each other and then we kiss.

Beyond the near cells, then, I notice one cell with its doors still shut. A number of Negro women are crowded against the bars, watching us. For a moment I stare at them. For a long and strange moment I feel an ancient awe. People in a cage! They seem to huddle there at a peculiar distance from me—castoffs. With a start I come to myself, trembling. The thought burns in my head: If, after all these days spent in a cage myself, I can feel this distance, how can I hope that others will learn to cross it? I hurry across the room. Others are walking over to that cell, too. We all clasp hands through the bars, exchange a few quick words—"Good luck . . . Take care . . . Freedom! Freedom!" Edie passes in to them some food she has left.

The wide barnlike door in the back of the room is still closed; apparently it won't be opened until all of us have gathered. My legs are weak and the bundle in my arms heavy, so I sit down on top of a large garbage can that stands by the door.

Now that door has been opened. Tony is standing near, and as he stares outside, into the world beyond this prison, and as he steps forward, I see his eyes change: light wakes in them again, reflecting the light of outdoors; they shine in his withered old man's cheeks. I sit there for a while still, facing into the prison room, and watch the eyes of each of my friends change as they move through the door.

FOURTEEN

I AM HOME again. It is still an extraordinary pleasure to perform the most ordinary motions—to sit up straight; to walk across a room or in and out of doors; to stare not at a wall but across distances; to breathe the living air.

I have left the Walk finally. When I joined it in October, my intention was to stay for only three weeks, but by the time the group began to run into trouble in Georgia, I felt too tied to these people to be able to leave. I am still—though I sit here now and they move on South through Florida. And I find even that I am bound, strangely, to all those who were involved in the struggle in Albany—helping us or contending against us.

Of course what we were attempting as we struggled was precisely to bind people together—or rather to bring them to recognize that we are, all of us, bound to each other and so should not deny this in our actions. One could say that nonviolence always tries to dramatize the words of St. Paul, "We are members one of another." It is hard to tell just how successful we were in bringing those with whom we struggled to feel this, but at any rate we have ended by feeling it ourselves—even painfully.

I sit and remember what it was like to leave Albany. On Monday, February 24, we walked out of the town. After a day and two nights of recuperation at Koinonia Farm nearby, even Yvonne, to my astonishment, was able to make the Walk—everybody but Candy, who had fallen

174]

sick. Her mother, who had come down to visit her and then stayed to help in the office, walked in her place. It took less than an hour, and we walked at a pace as slow as that which one sometimes takes in dreams. First Brad and Edie and Yvonne and Tyrone and Tony made the four-block circuit into the once forbidden shopping area. "It was very strange," Yvonne said later. "It was so highly stylized. The sidewalks there were almost deserted—I think Pritchett had cleared them. People peered out at us from doors or from windows, but nobody said a word to us. We walked in utter silence. And it was all so simple, finally, the action we were taking. It felt like pure symbol." Then all of us together moved out of town along the north side of Oglethorpe Avenue, A. J. leading the line. I stared at the legs of Mary Suzuki, who walked ahead of me. They were like queer whittled wooden legs carrying her along, and I thought: we are just barely managing this. Here there were more people on the streets. The townspeople who watched us pass, though hardly friendly, watched at least with little sign of the fear that often contorts their faces (who could fear us?), and very few that day cried out any words of abuse; they watched, it seemed to me, with a kind of awe at our condition. Would it possibly make any of them think a little about what we had been struggling for?

We had hardly started up the avenue when I saw that some message was being passed down along the line, and our slow file stopped. A few minutes before, I had seen Edie and Yvonne cross the street to begin to pass out leaflets on that side, and one of the cops escorting us, Assistant Chief Friend, had just ordered them brusquely back across the street, saying they would be allowed to pass out leaflets only along the sidewalk on which the rest of us walked. I looked around and saw Edie and Yvonne standing at the curb and Friend standing by them. All three figures looked stubborn. Edie and Yvonne had objected, saying that we always passed out leaflets on both sides of the street and there had been no prohibition of this included in the agreement we had reached with the city. Michele and Kit, seeing no one passing out leaflets across the street, had crossed over too and been stopped, and had made the same objection. Now A. J. was putting through a telephone call to Pritchett—who was in his office; he had decided not to accompany us this day, though he had done so on two earlier occasions. We stood and waited while the call was made.

It was a chilly morning, and as we held our places there in line I began to shiver. Erica put her hand on my shoulder, saying, "Take it easy." I told her, "I'm just cold," but perhaps it was fear that made me tremble, too, though I told myself that it wasn't. I glanced at Edie and Yvonne again. Neither of them, at the group meeting we had held in the jail, had joined Erica in suggesting that we consider a third battle with the authorities here. Nevertheless, we now stood on the verge of that third battle, and they had been quick to accept the challenge, and so had Kit and Michele. Later, each of them reported that it was a complete surprise to her to find she was ready, if our right to pass out leaflets freely was refused, to sit down on the sidewalk and begin everything all over again.

But if it had been Pritchett's idea to put us to this test—and not merely a misunderstanding on the part of Chief Friend—*he* decided now not to resume the struggle. After a few long minutes, word came that we could pass out our leaflets on both sides of the street, and the Walk moved slowly forward again.

At the edge of town we crossed a bridge over the Flint River. At the sight of the free waters below swirling downstream, I began to cry with relief; and as we approached the project cars that were waiting for us at the town line, many of us were crying.

We returned to Koinonia Farm, and for several weeks the walkers rested before setting out on the road again. But after a few days I got on a bus to begin my trip home. It was a strange ride, for the bus itself plunged through changing scenes, but though I was its passenger and carried along, I sat all the while thinking: This motion is unreal and I am not in fact moving from the place where I have been; for I could feel on my very flesh—as one feels sharp reality—those cords that still held me *there*.

They held me bound still to the friends with whom I had gone to jail. "Never go to jail with anyone," we had agreed, saying goodbye, because if you do, when you have to leave each other it is as though your own limbs were being torn from you. (Riding away from jail the afternoon we were released, I had sat next to John Papworth, whom I had never even seen face to face before that day, and without thinking we had each reached for the other's hand and held to it tightly on the trip back to headquarters.)

They held me bound still to the people of the Negro community of Albany, whose situation we had in some small measure shared during the two months we spent there, in and out of jail—those of us who were white better able now to imagine ourselves in their places, and they better able to feel close to us. Before I left I had driven into town to say goodbye to C. B. and Jack especially and to some of the other people whom I had met in the neighborhood or at mass meetings before I went into jail. I had wanted to say goodbyes; I had also wanted to hear what they would have to say about what we had accomplished or failed to accomplish in wresting from the city the compromise agreement that we had. Dave reported that after our release Marion Page had said to

[177

him, "This is the first split in the Rock of Gibraltar." He had smiled and added, "I wouldn't say that the rock has exactly crumbled, but the way I remember these things, the first split is the important one." I felt that I had to hear him say this myself, and to hear the reaction of others. Dave reported too that many people were elated about the outcome of the voter-registration demonstrations, which they had staged as planned that afternoon. The friends who met us at the jail's back door to drive us home had told us as we climbed into the cars that picketers were out in front of the jail and in front of the county jail across the street and the federal courthouse—and that Pritchett had as yet made no move to stop them. Before the day was out a series of small groups, in all fifty people, had carried their signs north of Oglethorpe, prepared to be jailed as they always had been in the past when they tried to demonstrate in that part of town. Not one person had been arrested. Yvonne had talked since to some students, who felt that a precedent had been set and that it was our actions which had won for them an important extension of their civil liberties; but she had talked to others who were less sure that the incident meant much and wondered whether the leniency shown to them that day would last.

As I talked, myself, to various people in town, most of them shrugged away the question about specific gains our actions may or may not have won for them. We had given them heart, for we had shown that the city *could* be budged. And one man told me, "Just the fact that you turned up in our midst and you were willing to make this fight—most of you white people—" He had a little difficulty in saying the words "white people," and he waved his hand then, clumsily, and ended, "That's the difference to us, too." We were standing outside and he indicated with a sudden gesture a nearby bush blowing slightly in the wind. "It's like suddenly seeing something before your eyes you didn't know was there—*could* be there. But I'm not saying it well." We both stared at the bush awkwardly.

I visited Marion Page. He told me, "You taught us something about tenacity. And," he added, "there's another reason I won't forget you all." He told me that he had attended the original Atlanta University, whose faculty was integrated, its student body partially so, all taking their meals together, living in the same dormitories; most of his teachers New Englanders. "I learned from them, at the time, to respect the white man's 'democracy in action.' Then I came back to Albany." He talked for a long while about the life here—and of those who hold the power and "use it and use it and use it"—and he told me of the deadly bitterness that had entered his soul. He raised his eyes and gave me a long look. "You people have given me back a part of myself that I had lost."

I wanted to say to him: And when you tell me that, you give me back, too, a part of myself of which all of us who are white have been stripped for too long. Later I stopped by at the headquarters of the Albany Movement, and when I said that I had come to say goodbye, a woman whom I had seen at mass meetings often but whose name I didn't know came forward, saying, "You can't really leave, you know; you belong to us now." I kept hearing her words that evening as my bus began to put miles between us—because she was right, I could not leave. Even sitting at this distance, home now, I have not been able to.

I am bound still, more than I thought I could be, to those in the white community of Albany with whom we contended for so many weeks, all those who as we passed along their streets, offering our leaflets, or knocked on their doors, seeking interviews, turned on us looks of such anxiety—sometimes controlled, sometimes desperate; and those who, acting on their behalf, under Pritchett's direction, tried to get rid of us for them, so they could put us out of mind. Because they turned the key on us in jail instead of letting us pass freely through their city, the people of the white community of Albany had finally to give us a great deal more of their attention, of course; but we on our part had to give a great deal of attention to them, too, and if we became finally a little more real to them, they certainly became more real to us. Trying as best we could to behave in ways that would make them feel they could *not* put us from them—and also that, as we were friendly, there was no need to—our own actions brought us daily closer to them, inevitably.

After the Walk had left Albany, Edie and Kit wrote, "Remaining in jail for almost two months is a strange way to acquire residency, but when we were released we felt we were not released from the city." They have now left the Walk, too, and returned to Albany from Florida, to set up an experimental project. They want to see what they can do, just as two concerned individuals who feel they do know a little about the city now, to open channels of communication between the Negro and the white communities. One thing that gives them hope is that some of the individuals within the white community whom they approached actually encouraged them to return. They will be playing a lonely role, however; they themselves may feel now as though they have become citizens of Albany, but most people in that city will still treat them as outsiders. They know this, of course. In an encounter like the one we lived through, we can hope to change a little those who oppose us—and that little can make a very practical difference; but they are not likely to be changed by our actions as much as we ourselves are changed. We tried in Albany, however clumsily, to act out the truth that all men are kin to one another. As the drama ended it was we ourselves, inevitably, who felt the truth of it most sharply—and felt it hard to simply take our leave.

For just a few days I returned to Albany myself, wanting to see how Kit and Edie's project was faring, and while I was there I dropped in at the city jail to see the Chief. He asked me into his office and we talked for a while. I told him that I was writing this book and would send him a copy and he said, "I'd appreciate that very much." Then as I got up to leave he said, "Take care of yourself, hear?" It was both hard not to laugh and hard not to cry at that command from him. Does even the Chief feel something of what we feel? Or was he simply relieved not to have us any longer in his care?

I have had to write this book because, like Edie and Kit, though I left Albany, I was not released from the city—or from all the people with whom our action there had involved us. But neither has writing it released me from them, and, still bound to them, I dedicate my book

to the thirty-five friends with whom I entered the Albany city jail,

to the people of the Negro community of Albany, whose lives we shared a little while we were there,

to Attorney C. B. King and Attorney Thomas Jackson, whose daily visits sustained us,

to A. J. Muste and Dave Dellinger and all those others who labored—in Albany and from a distance—to get us out,

and to all those who put us in there—chief among them, Laurie Pritchett.

You are more real to me than I have been able to make you in these prison notes.

THESE were the friends with whom I entered the Albany
city jail:

Ross Anderson, 63, of Greenville, South Carolina. Served
   four days, first jail-in; released part of the time on his own
   recognizance because of his age.
Carl Arnold, 21, of Atlanta, Georgia. Served twenty-four
   days, first jail-in.
Bob Barber, 29, of Kalamazoo, Michigan. Served eight
   days, first jail-in.
Barry Bassin, 19, of Brooklyn, New York. Served nineteen
   days, second jail-in.
Tony Brown, 27, of San Francisco, California. Served
   twenty-four days, first jail-in; twenty-seven days, second
   jail-in.
Allen Cooper, 25, of Albuquerque, New Mexico. Served
   twenty-four days, first jail-in; six days, second jail-in; then
   paid fine after three trips to the hospital.
Marv Davidov, 32, of St. Paul, Minnesota. Served twenty-
   seven days, second jail-in.
Phil Davis. S.N.C.C. field worker, not a member of the
   Walk, but jailed with Yvonne on January 23 for picketing
   a fallout-shelter "test"; out on bail after seven days and
   never called to trial.
Dave Dellinger, 48, of Glen Gardner, New Jersey. Served
   eight days, first jail-in.
Ralph Di Gia, 49, of New York City. Served twenty-seven
   days, second jail-in.
Erica Enzer, 38, of Chicago, Illinois. Served twenty-four
   days, first jail-in; twenty-seven days, second jail-in.

[183

MICHELE GLOOR, 20, of Northbrook, Illinois. Served twenty-five days, first jail-in; twenty-seven days, second jail-in.

PETER GREGONIS, 38, of Silverton, Oregon. Served eighteen days, first jail-in (then bailed out to await appeal of the case to a higher court); served twenty-seven days, second jail-in.

KATHERINE HAVICE, 23, of Boulder, Colorado. Served twenty-four days, first jail-in; twenty-seven days, second jail-in.

TYRONE JACKSON, 19, of Albany, Georgia. Served twenty-four days, first jail-in; twenty-seven days, second jail-in.

GENE KEYES, 22, of Champaign, Illinois. Served twenty-seven days, second jail-in.

YVONNE MATHEWS KLEIN, 30, of Minneapolis, Minnesota. Served twenty-five days, first jail-in; thirty-one days, second jail-in.

CANDY KRICKER, 17, of Woodstock, New York. Served eight days, first jail-in; nineteen days, second jail-in.

PETER LIGHT, 20, of Vancouver, British Columbia. Served four days, second jail-in.

BRADFORD LYTTLE, 36, of Voluntown, Connecticut. Served twenty-four days, first jail-in; nineteen days, second jail-in.

KENNETH MEISTER, 39, of Voluntown, Connecticut. Served twenty-seven days, second jail-in.

FRED MOORE, 22, of California. Not a member of the Walk, but served two days, first jail-in. A friend of the walkers, passing through Albany on his way to Florida to spend Christmas with his family, he went to the jail to inquire about the arrests, and was held himself, for investigation.

RONALD MOOSE, 18, of High Point, North Carolina. Served ten days, second jail-in; after a death in his family, paid fine so as to return home.

MICHAEL NEWMAN, 19, of Vancouver, British Columbia, Canada. Served nineteen days, second jail-in.

ALAN NYYSOLA, 22, of Baltimore, Maryland. Served twenty-four days, first jail-in; nineteen days, second jail-in.

JOHN PAPWORTH, 42, of London, England. Served eight days, second jail-in.

ERIC ROBINSON, 20, of Lompoc, California. Served twenty-five days, first jail-in; nineteen days, second jail-in.

RAY ROBINSON, JR., 28, of Washington, D. C. Served twenty-four days, first jail-in; twenty-seven days, second jail-in.

EDITH MAE SNYDER, 22, of Brooklyn, New York. Served twenty-five days, first jail-in; twenty-seven days, second jail-in.

JOHN STEPHENS, 20, of San Diego, California. Served twenty-seven days, second jail-in.

WILLIAM SUPERNAW, 25, of New York City. Served several days, second jail-in; after a death in his family, paid fine so as to return home.

MARY SUZUKI, 26, of Montreal, Quebec, Canada. Served nineteen days, second jail-in.

JOE TUCHINSKY, 27, of Chicago, Illinois. Served five days, first jail-in; coordinated activities at headquarters, second jail-in.

AL UHRIE, 32, of Glen Gardner, New Jersey. Served twelve days, first jail-in.

CRAIG WORSOE, 21, of Alaska. Served seven days, second jail-in; then taken to hospital for emergency appendectomy, after which he paid fine and left Albany.

The Quebec-Washington-Guantanamo Walk for Peace began in the city of Quebec on May 26, 1963. After covering about 2,800 miles—and with delays while walkers served jail sentences in Griffin, Macon and Albany, Georgia—it reached Miami, Florida, on May 29, 1964. On October 27, 1964—after lengthy preparations—six of the walkers attempted to sail the power boat *Spirit of Freedom* to Havana, Cuba. The United States government seized the boat, claiming violation of the McCarran Act. It then filed action in federal district court in Miami to complete the confiscation, and the Florida American Civil Liberties Union agreed to plead for the walkers—the case being aptly entitled *The United States of America* v. *The Spirit of Freedom*.

PHOTOGRAPHS
ALBANY, GEORGIA 1964
SENECA, NEW YORK 1983

1964

courtesy of Irwin Klein

Ray, Marv, Tom

Near Athens, Georgia

Passing out leaflets in Georgia

Michele and Kit

courtesy of Committee on Nonviolent Action Bulletin

courtesy of Consuelo Kanaga

Meeting: Edie, Gene, Alan N., Joe, Ron, Candy, Yvonne, Ralph, Barbara, Brad, Erica

Tyrone and Ray

courtesy of *Consuelo Kanaga*

courtesy of Consuelo Kanaga

Second arrest in Albany

Assistant Chief Friend arresting Brad at the air base, Albany

courtesy of Committee on Nonviolent Action Bulletin

Ray arrested in
Macon

Yvonne arrested
in Albany

courtesy of Larry Bevis, Albany Journal

courtesy of Consuelo Kanaga

Barbara arrested
in Albany

Edie arrested in
Macon

Michele

Yvonne,
Edie, and
Barbara

Erica

Michele, Tony

Mary

Edie

Yvonne

Ralph, John, Candy, and Carl

courtesy of Clifford Vaughs, Student Nonviolent Coordinating Committee

Candy, Barbara

Marv and Alan N.

courtesy of Clifford Vaughs, Student Nonviolent Coordinating Committee

courtesy of Clifford Vaughs, Student Nonviolent Coordinating Committee

John

Brad

courtesy of Clifford Vaughs, Student Nonviolent Coordinating Committee

Eric

courtesy of Clifford Vaughs, Student Nonviolent Coordinating Committee

Allen Cooper, John-i-thin

courtesy of Clifford Vaughs, Student Nonviolent Coordinating Committee

courtesy of Committee on Nonviolent Action Bulletin

Walking the forbidden streets in downtown Albany. In the picture at upper left, Dave Dellinger is observing. In the picture at upper right, A.J. Muste is out front.

courtesy of Committee on Nonviolent Action Bulletin

Tony

1983

CHRONOLOGY
BY BLUE LUNDEN

JULY 25: Barbara arrived with Rhea at Northwoods in upstate New York. They joined Blue and Quinn on the 21st day of their walk from New York City to Seneca.

JULY 26: Barbara walked from Trumansburg to Ovid Center, N.Y. with Blue, Quinn, Rhea, and Donna.

JULY 28: Walk was joined Jun Song, Terri, Lisa, and Kitrinka. The entire group reached the Encampment that afternoon.

JULY 29: We spent most of the day at camp and joined Jun Song for part of her daily walk around the Army depot.

JULY 30: We joined with 75 other women in New York City Women's Pentagon Action's Feminist Walk, from Seneca Falls to the Encampment. In the town of Waterloo, a mob blocked our way at the bridge. We sat to diffuse potential violence and to insist on our constitutional right to pass. 54 women were arrested and taken to the local jail.

JULY 31: We were transported at 5 a.m. from jail to the Interlaken Junior High School and were held in the cafeteria for five days, as we refused to give our names or cooperate in any way with this illegal arrest. Women from the Encampment began vigiling outside the school and are harassed by local townspeople. The governor declared a "state of emergency" and state police were brought in.

AUGUST 3: We were taken to the Seneca County Fair Grounds to a barn that had been converted to a courtroom. After processing 14 or us individually, each of whom refused to give her name and most of whom refused to walk, the judge finally yielded to our demand to be heard as a group. We were all brought in and allowed to make our statement. Charges were dismissed and even our fingerprints and mug shots were returned to us. We returned to the Encampment, where Barbara spent another week before returning home.

The Women's Encampment for a Future of Peace and Justice continues and can be reached at:

Box 5440, Route 96
Romulus, NY 14541
607-869-5825

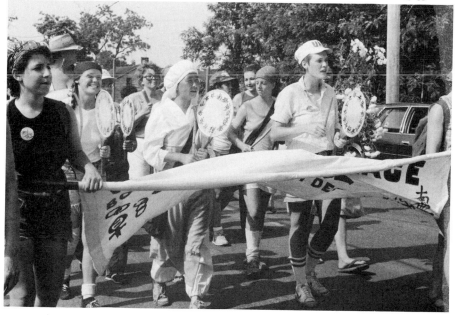

Jun Song (center), other Buddhist women walking with their drums from Boston to the Encampment

Front lawn of the Seneca Women's Encampment, Romulus, NY

A workshop meeting by the dome

Circle of women listening

Walk from Seneca Falls to honor women's history

Sign on a garage in the Village of Waterloo, NY

At the bridge, shaking American flags

Man with a rifle is disarmed by police

Barbara holding her flag/bouquet of wildflowers

Men yelling at the women on the walk

Barbara sitting down in a circle at the bridge with Quinn (l) and Blue (r)

One of the seated women is arrested for disorderly conduct

As she is being arrested, Barbara blows a kiss to tearful Jun Song

Barbara is handcuffed

Grace (center) and other women circling in support of
the 54 arrested women at the school/jail in Interlaken

Jane (left) talks with the townspeople at the jail

The Jane Does testify at the arraignment at the Seneca County Fairgrounds

In the courtroom, waiting for the decision

Back at the Encampment, Barbara with the flag pole point

One of the all-women circles at the peace camp in front of the barn

SENECA WRITINGS
1984

A NEW SPIRIT
MOVES AMONG US

Dear Norma — I've just read the text of a talk you gave about feminist organizing in the peace movement.[1] You are dismayed by the women-only actions more and more women take part in these days — or rather, dismayed by the spirit in which they (we) join these actions. A spirit, you feel, that is different from the spirit that moved women to band together in earlier days. I agree with you that a new spirit moves among us. I took part in some of the actions called by Women Strike for Peace in the sixties and yes, the WISP style, for example, was a different style. Though I think I can see some seeds, in that style, of this new style that alarms you. I want to try to speak to your fears. I was at the Seneca Women's Peace Camp last summer for two weeks (five of those days I spent in a local jail, but with 53 women from the camp, so I count them as days at the camp). Because I've not the energies I once had, I hadn't taken part in a large action for some time and went to Seneca unsure of what I would experience there. I came away filled not with misgivings about this new spirit that moves us, but with a deeper hopefulness — because of it — than I have ever known.

You visited the camp too, I know — for we greeted each other. But it was a one-day visit, I think. I can't help wishing it had been longer. For ah, Norma, I have to say: You don't know us very well. I say this to you not harsely but in the spirit of the friendship we have kept for many years. A friendship rooted — wouldn't you say? — in our shared commitment to struggle against violence wherever we find it, as best we know how. And our shared belief that this best way will always be a way that is not in itself violent.

It is clear to me, of course, that you feel that in joining the women-only actions I have, as it were, *lost* my way. For you feel that these actions contain at their core the element of violence, of hatefulness. You say that those of us who take them "manifest, to a greater or lesser degree, an anti-male attitude"; "There is an aversion to acknowledging that (men) too can be victims"; "Maleness is...defined" among us "as a social evil"; and we see ourselves as building toward a future that is "women only", rejects "one half of the species." *You* adhere, you say, "to a perspective that holds that the bond between male and female is biological...fundamental and inescapable." You add, "Unlike the class struggle, the battle between the sexes cannot be characterized as...irreconcilable...Unless we are prepared to postulate a genetic origin for masculine aggression...we must look to culture as the main determinant of the masculine mystique ...(And) human beings possess the capacity to go beyond the limits imposed by cultural norms."

So many words rush up in me. Where to begin? Let me begin by saying that I am puzzled by the distinction you draw between class struggle and battle between the sexes — the one conflict irreconcilable, you say, but the other not. I don't understand. Why can't one describe the two battles in very comparable terms? In class struggle, the battle is with an owner class which feels it has the right to exploit the labor of another class, the working class — treats that class as one of the properties it owns. In the battle between the sexes, battle is with those men who feel they have the right as a *gender* class to ownership privileges; feel that, even when they own nothing else in the whole world, they do own women — own our labor, even when they don't pay for that labor; own our very bodies, our sexuality. The struggle is in both cases — isn't it? — to assert in action that no one has the right to own another person? And if this struggle is nonviolent, it involves, doesn't it, a refusal to cooperate with the abusers, an attempt to destroy their authority — I mean their authority *as* abusers; but also a refusal to try to destroy them as persons. So — how is the one struggle any more reconcilable than the other, or any less so? The point being to destroy capitalism, and the point being to destroy patriarchy — and not, in either case, to destroy the individuals who behave as though capitalism, as though patriarchy, were legitimate systems of relating to one another.

I'm forgetting to speak to your underlying fear, though, aren't I? You are afraid that our struggle is *not* a nonviolent struggle. Afraid that we *are* willing to destroy the patriarchs as individuals. You see us as trying to build toward a future that is women only. Ah, Norma — do I really have to assure you that we don't contemplate trying to kill off men? I'll confess that it makes me angry to have to write out the words of this grotesque question. It makes me angry to have to repeat, repeat, repeat: We don't hate men, we hate the clearly hateful things that men have done to us, are still doing to us — hate it that they rape us, batter us, exploit us, empoverish us, silence us. Well — it is too simple to say that we don't hate them. Of course we sometimes hate them. Don't you? But we also hate to hate them. And we often love them — love them, in fact, even *as* we hate them. They are, after all, flesh of our flesh. We give birth to them. Are born of the same mothers. Are fathered by them. Now and then, yes, I do encounter a woman who has been so harmed by men that she likes to daydream, out loud, about a world without them. When I remember all the battered women I have met — and the millions

I don't know; all the raped women I know — and the millions I don't know; when I remember the threat men pose to the very life of the planet — I can feel tempted to take psychic refuge in that daydream, myself. For a moment or so. Call it battle fatigue. But I can assure you: the spirit of the Seneca encampment is not the spirit of that despairing daydream.

When we come together in our women-only circles it is not to try to deny our bond with men; it is to *affirm* our bond with one another. The bond between male and female — yes, of course, it is fundamental. But let me add, Norma: It is not under any threat. It never has been. The bond that *has* been under threat — for centuries and centuries, for all the centuries of the patriarchy — is the bond between women and women. This bond, too, is fundamental. And biological. (Isn't it?) But we have been *forbidden* to affirm it. Our gathering together as we do now amounts in effect to civil disobedience — whether or not we decide, while together, to climb some military fence, block some entrance, commit some act for which we can be sent to jail. For the First Commandment patriarchy expects women to obey is: THOU SHALT BOND WITH MEN — AND MEN *only*. THOU SHALT BOND WITH NO OTHER. (We are allowed to bond with "their" children, of course, but — to bond with them only *as* "their" children.) It's not irrelevant, I think, that you should have used the word "inescapable" to describe our relation to men. For they have tried to make a natural bond into something more than that — or rather, less than that: tried to make it bondage. The word "bond" itself is a tricky one, I find. I have just looked it up in the dictionary. "That which binds or restrains; fetter, shackle…confinement." Though a little later: "that which binds, joins…connecting link…" There really should be two distinct words, shouldn't there? — one for the link which does not confine, one for the link which does? The fact that there are *not* two words says much about the patriarchy.

I believe, myself, that as we women find our courage to affirm our bond with one another, we will in that very process become free also to *truly* affirm our bond with men — our *natural* bond with them, rather than the bondage we have been forced to *pretend* is natural. But men, or most men, find it difficult to imagine this possibility. When they imagine us breaking out of bondage to them, they can only imagine our breaking away from them altogether. Which explains, no doubt, why they never invented two words in place of the single word "bond". When we women gather together — for more than card games or certain "good works"; when we give each other deep attention — men interpret our turning to one another as a turning *against them*. As abandonment. Or worse: a conspiracy to kill them off. And this should make it clear, by the way, why when we turn to one another we *have* to do so in women-only space. If men are present, it is very simply too distracting to have to cope with their anxiety. And with our own anxiety *about* their anxiety.

Their anxiety can take scary forms. It took scary forms at Seneca last summer. For if we didn't have to deal with it within the camp, we had to deal with it in the form of harassment from without — harassment from men in the surrounding towns; and yes, the women with them, too — afraid as you are afraid, dear friend, that when we choose to give this deep attention to one another, we do violence to the men, and we become a threat. "Nuke the bitches!" "Nuke the lezzies!" *Their* fear of us led them to yell. And they had t-shirts made up with these words lettered on them — so the words could be uttered non-stop. They yelled other words at us, too, of course. "Commies!" was as frequent a yell. But it was more apt to be "Go home, commies!" Lezzies had to be nuked.

"Lesbian." You never use the word even once in your talk. But you do say that a sound approach to organizing "would not inject lifestyle preferences...into political projects." And I assume that when you say this you have

in mind very specifically the lesbian "lifestyle preference."
I assume too that you think of the new spirit among us
which so disturbs you as essentially a lesbian spirit. It
may be accurate to name it that. Though it is a spirit
acted out by many women who are not lesbians. We lesbians perhaps were the first — or were a majority among
the first — to allow ourselves to begin to act it out, with
a new daring. A daring to trust ourselves to one another
in an extraordinary way — before making our political
choices. To listen, listen to one another; share with each
other thoughts that would usually be guarded, feelings
that would usually be guarded — even from ourselves. To
open ourselves to one another — and so to our own deeper
selves — in ways that in earlier times we could only have
dared to open ourselves with a lover. I wonder: will you
frown as you read these words — "with a lover?"

"The Beloved Community." You remember *those* words,
of course, from the sixties — words used in the Black nonviolent movement to describe the community they, we,
(all of us committed to nonviolence) were trying to bring
into being. Not just in some far away future but right
now, as best we could. I would say that that name describes very precisely the world these women who so
alarm you are trying to bring into being — in their, our,
own way. A new way, but a way that owes very much
to that earlier movement.

But why does it have to be a new way? Why can't it
remain that older way — taken by women *and* men?
Didn't I taste community among my comrades of the
sixties — comrades in the various nonviolent actions I
joined against racism, poverty, imperialism, war? Yes,
I did, Norma. And that remembered taste can make me
at times impatient for the day when our circles of women
will widen to include men. And yet — I feel more and
more sure that we are right for a time to keep our circles
of action women-only circles. More and more sure that
if we do, the circles we form some day that include us all

194]

will more nearly deserve the name of "beloved community." For though I did, yes, share much with those earlier comrades, much, too, was left *un*shared among us.
I, for example, never told them that I was a lesbian.
Shared this with only one comrade — a black man who
was in love with me. Shared it with *him* only out of anxiety that his pride not be hurt by my failure to fall in love
with him in return. Though my own experience as a
member of a despised group had surely much to do with
my taking part in the struggles of the sixties, I remained
discreetly silent about my own oppressed state, fearing
that if I spoke of it my speaking might create a hateful
distance between me and the very people with whom I
felt identified — identified precisely because of that unmentionable state. I struggled alongside comrades with whom
I felt bonded and yet not bonded — some part of me always in shadow. Others kept other parts of their deep
selves in shadow.

And what did this matter? you may ask. What did it
matter if some parts of us remained in shadow? If we
could all agree that racism must end, that the war against
Vietnam must end, that poverty must end, etc., etc.,
what matter? Here was bonding enough to enable us to
fight the necessary fight. But I don't agree. It was not
enough. Or we would have made an even greater difference than we did make. We made a difference. Those
were extraordinary struggles. I'm proud to have taken
part in them. And proud of the company I kept. But
nonviolent struggle is always in the process of invention.
Wouldn't you agree, Norma — that it has still to be further and further invented? I think that we are further
inventing it in our all-women circles. And that the very
much deeper sharing of our selves which we are learning
is at the very heart of this invention.

I know that you are concerned — passionately concerned — that the peace movement be a mass movement.
It must be a movement, you stress toward the end of your

[195

talk, "embracing women with widely differing viewpoints on every conceivable issue." And so it must design actions that will "reach out to the broadest possible spectrum of that constituency." I know that you are anxious because you see actions like those carried out at Seneca as bound to attract simply a very special segment of the population. It is perfectly true that there are a great many women who would not — presently — dream of turning up at a women-only peace camp. Though it is also true that the idea of these camps — born, as you know, at Greenham Common in England — is proving to be very very contagious. I find I can hardly keep up with the word of new ones coming into being — around this country and around the world. And my own conviction is that the sharing process with which we experiment in these camps is, in fact, the surest way to work toward the very mass movement that you want. Because it is the surest way to build trust between women with "widely differing viewpoints."

There may be faster ways to move toward a mass movement. But I know that you would agree that the point is not simply to have numbers on our side. If we took as a *goal* the creation of a mass movement, I think we could end up with — well, just that: a great many people, a mass of people, able to move in saying very simple "No's" together — "No's" to things-as-they-are; but not a mass at all enabled to begin to bring into being Beloved Communities, truly new ways of living together. If, instead, we concentrate upon trying to invent together better ways of listening to one another as we make decisions — ways of listening that deny none of our differences — I think we begin to create a new world even as we do this. And I think that this caring process can release among us our very deepest powers.

But it is time that I began to try to describe to you my own experience of this empowerment. Let me attempt a narrative of the days I spent last summer at Seneca. I can't help feeling that if you had been there as I was for all those days — and most especially if you had been there with us the five days we spent in jail — you would have lost your fear of what happens in our circles.

Two dear friends, Quinn and Blue, had set out to walk to Seneca from New York City, and I'd decided to join their walk for the last two days. So I'd flown to New York, then hitched a ride with another friend who wanted to walk with them, Rhea. We'd rendezvoused at Northwoods, the lesbian farming household near Ithaca — at day's end, July 26th; and started out early the next morning from Trumansburg, about 19 or 20 miles from the camp. Blue and Quinn wore the small cloth signs: WOMENS PEACE WALK, NYC TO SENECA ARMY DEPOT that had helped them enter dialogue with the people they'd met along their way. I wore the slit-down-the-sides orange pillowslip which read WEAPONS THAT CAN DESTROY ALL LIFE CANNOT DEFEND US, and on the back: NONVIOLENT STRUGGLE IS THE ONLY REALISM.

It felt good to be on the road like this again. Yes, it recalled the miles I had walked in the sixties. Our signs speaking in one way. Our feet speaking without words. Speaking our refusal to sit still and let things stay as they are. Speaking our dismay and speaking our hopes. Blue and Quinn had learned a song from the women at Northwoods which we slow-chanted: WALK, WALK, WALK FOR PEACE. WALK OVER THE LAND — a stride taken for each accented word. By the side of the road wildflowers gleamed: chicory, the most delicate and luminous of blues. The sweet flat-headed Queen Anne's Lace. Fields of huge farm-grown sunflowers. Beautiful ruddy faces. Blue and Quinn spoke of how, during their walk, their sense of the land had deepened. And their sense of the danger in which it lay. Yes, as we set our feet down, we remembered: This is what is threatened by the warmakers. All of this. Not our lives alone. As we set our feet down — in long steps — I can remember thinking, without words: We will not agree that this belongs to them to destroy. We will not agree. For we are of this earth, and we will not agree that it belongs to them to destroy.

It had been a long while since I'd walked more than a mile or so. And I wasn't sure how well I would hold up. I walked more easily than I'd expected — these deep feelings perhaps carrying me along. But by mid-day I was ready for a rest. Joined Rhea, who was taking her turn as driver-of-the-car. And then we all paused for a picnic on the lawn of the High School at Interlaken; and I took a long nap there under a large shade tree. It later seemed curious that we had chosen just this place for our longest stop. This was the school that, four days later, would become the improvised jail for fifty four of us. I remember staring up into the leaves of the great tree, before pulling a blanket round me and shutting my eyes. Thinking again: We must refuse. We must refuse.

Later in the day (I was walking again) a car approached from the direction of the camp, stopped, and an old friend jumped out and ran up to me to embrace me, embrace us all: Kady. Whom I hadn't seen in too many years. Grown skinnier with age, as I had. More wrinkled, as I had. We stared at one another. Half laughing. Half crying. She touched my arms — "It's you." "And you," I said, touching her sunburned arms. (She'd been working there at the camp since its opening.) And then she told me that she had prepared a special tent for me. I'd been worrying that I might not be able to quite take camping conditions. For I have become, at this point in my life, freakishly susceptible to the cold. But she told me that she'd heard of my worrying, and she and still another friend, Maureen, had built for me — out of four by fours and plywood — a simple sturdy raised bed, with foam rubber mattress; and they'd collected extra blankets, too. So I needn't worry. Needn't stay outside the grounds. And Kady hopped back into her car and was off — back to work. (Work on a system of boardwalks to make the camp accessible to disabled women.) And I walked on, blessed — miles from the camp still, but welcomed already.

The next day we received another welcome, though still on the road. Donna, a friend from California headed for the camp, had arrived at Northwoods now; so four of us set out that last morning. And we'd walked only a mile or so when, at a crossroads, we saw a small band of smiling women waiting for us — Jun Song, the Buddhist monk from Japan, who had walked to the encampment from Boston in early summer, and three young American women who had walked with her — Terry, Lisa, Katrinka. The women bowed to us, the grave Buddhist bow, hands together. We returned the bow. For days now, each day, they had been walking the twelve miles round the Army depot, carrying their banner: WALK FOR PEACE ROUND THE SENECA ARMY DEPOT. CIVILIZATION IS NOT NUCLEAR WAR AND KILLING AND NUCLEAR BOMBS. CIVILIZATION IS MUTUAL AFFECTION AND RESPECT FOR EACH OTHER. But on this morning they had decided to rise very early and walk instead to meet us; then walk back with us to the camp. Jun Song, after an intent glance into my face, hurried over to me, and began to knead the tired muscles of my back with her quick strong hands. Then she bowed to me again. And I to her — with astonished thanks. And we set forth again.

The Buddhists had round flat drums, which they beat as they cried out their chant: NA-MU-MYO-HO-REN-GE-KYO! Which cannot quite be translated, Lisa told us, but is a cry for peace, a cry which declares that peace is the needed way. I felt tears rise in me as we strode along together. Felt: Yes, this is the way to walk — with the concentrated attention which is prayer. Jun Song handed me her drum and I practiced, learned the distinctive beat: two quick, five slow strokes. "It is the beat of our hearts," Terry said. We were passing lovely fields of corn,

[199

grains. I began to strike my drum in greeting to the fields. In greeting to the birds that skimmed above them. And all the life around us — threatened life around us. To greet it with the life pulse of our drums. Affirming: It is one heartbeat; we are all one. And affirming: We refuse to have our lives set at naught. I began when a car would speed by us, too fast, or an army helicopter to whir high in the air above us, to beat out: We refuse this. We'll be no part of this. To beat out exorcism. It occurred to me suddenly that this double statement I felt I could make with the drum was the double statement which is the strength of nonviolent struggle: the repeated refusal to give violence our obedient allegiance; the repeated insistence upon our kinship with all life. Even of course the lives of those by whom we felt threatened. The strokes with which it felt to me as though I could almost strike from the violent ones their deadly energies, seemed not like an assault upon them but like a healing — stripping away from them that which was deadly to them as well as to us.

At our lunch break, Jun Song spread a cloth upon the ground, told me to lie down, gave me a kneading this time from head to toes — and also a pummeling, with hard but careful fists. I'd taken some time-out from walking in the morning, but after her drubbing found myself able to walk the remaining miles without another break.

Cars and bikes had brought a number of other women from the camp to join us on our final lap. We agreed to walk in silence, except for the drums, which would speak for us. Walked now past miles of military fencing. Here was the grim Army Depot at last. Blue and Quinn glanced at one another — their long hike near its end. A jeep full of military guards began to follow us, inside the fence. We turned toward them so that they could read our signs. And drummed: We want no part of this; drummed: We want no part of this. At the Depot's main gate we stopped and drummed and drummed. The men on guard there staring at us through the wire. Their eyes sometimes dreamy, it seemed to me. Did the drums put them in touch with some disobedient heartbeat in themselves? We could hope so.

Then through the small town of Romulus — American flags stuck out in front of a lot of the houses. As defense against us. From one of the passing cars, a man yelled, "Fuck you up the ass!" Gave us the finger. Jun Song, her round face calm, uttered again her measured passionate cry — voice breaking on the final REN-GE-KYO, I mused, a little as the mourning dove's voice breaks in the final notes of its call. And then women were running down the road toward us. For, just ahead, was the encampment. On the lawn in front of the old farmhouse, we formed a circle. Circle of greeting. Sang for a while. Stared into one another's faces. Blue's face, Quinn's face, were shining. They nodded at me.

Kady was in the circle, and she took me now to see my comfortable tent — in the section for disabled women. An easy walk to the sheds and tents where workshops would be held, easy walk to the outdoors kitchen area. After I'd rested a while — marvelling still as I lay there at my newly-constructed bed — she led me on a tour of the rest of the camp: the clinic, the barn with video projector, the sign-up-for-work shed, the kitchen sheds and fire-pits, the cold pits for food, the sinks, the portable toilets; and then the two back fields, crowded with a wonderful variety of tents and teepees, the one field for women without children, the other for women with children. The children running about in happy grubby-faced freedom.

I was delighted at the looks of the children. I was delighted, too, at the looks of the women, both young and old, moving across the stubbly ground here at one task or another. Did you feel any of this delight? I wonder. They seemed to me to move with a lovely independence of spirit — or at least motion toward independence. The sturdy among them touching in one way. (In earlier days, I mused, I had rarely seen women so at ease in their bodies.) The frailer ones, or the disabled, touching in still another way. But no—not in another way, in just the same way: each seeming to have learned, or to be learning, not to despise her body—as we have all been taught to—but to discover in it new capabilities. On August first, the day of the mass civil disobedience actions at the Depot, one woman on crutches and two blind women went over the fence. Perhaps you saw this on video, as I did. I was told that one of the military guards cried out in panic to Marianne, the woman on crutches: "Lady, why are you doing this?" And unhappily several of the demonstrators themselves cried out to the blind women, Sara and Diane, "You can't do that! You're blind!" But they could. And they did. This was the prevailing spirit at the camp, I'd say: We can and we will.

I was surprised at the variety of women who had been attracted to the action. There were very few women of color, as I'm sure you noted. And I hope the organizers are asking themselves why. And asking women of color that question, — and listening hard to their answers.

But we were women of many ages. And the difference in the kinds of lives we'd been living was considerable. This would become evident in the workshops—and as we sat about the outdoor fires, questioning one another.

What most moved me was the fact that in spite of the differences among us, and in spite of our numbers, and in spite of the fact that our population kept shifting—new women arriving all the time, others having to leave, the small staff and a few stubborn volunteers the only long-term inhabitants—the commitment was to making decisions by consensus. And this process was not abandoned. Sometimes, it's true, the process was rushed—and so became a shadow of itself. This was so at the general meeting held the first evening I arrived. The staff was feeling some panic, I think—for August first was drawing near. I can't remember now what we were being asked to decide, but I remember that too little time was allowed for us to listen to one another. I remember Blue, by my side, was shaking her head: "Shouldn't do it this way."

The wonder to me was that in so many other instances real listening did take place. Ways kept being found to enable this to happen. More and more of these ways need to be invented — and are being invented. I think for example of a meeting at which the issue was raised as to whether in encounters with the press and with people from the surrounding towns we should try to play down the fact that many of us were lesbians. When the discussion began, consensus seemed unlikely. Those on the one side and those on the other appeared decided. Voices were strained. I could see that each side felt judged by the other. Donna suggested that we try what she called the "fishbowl" way of listening to one another. Women who were lesbians should form one circle, women who were heterosexual another. A few women spoke up to say they thought of themselves as neither or both, so she suggested that they form a third circle. Each group, as its time came, would become a circle within the circle of others — and take uninterrupted turns within this smaller round, to speak their feelings. And so we did. Without fear of judgment now, because speaking with those with whom we felt most at east — while the others listened in. And so speaking more deeply than before. When we formed one large circle again, the talk was no longer strained. We really had heard one another. And consensus, to the astonishment of all, I think, was reached easily. That consensus: We would be more likely to calm the fears of townspeople if we spoke without fear ourselves.

I remember especially of the final round of this meeting the look on the face of a neatly-dressed church woman — as she told us that she'd never before given any thought to the subject of lesbians or homophobia. "But," she said, "I do want to open myself to new thoughts." I think that the form we had chosen for this meeting had helped her to want just that. The look on her face was a look of grave surprise.

I remember, too, another meeting — a workshop improvised one day on the subject of fear of sexual intimacy. A few of us, sitting round one of the fire-pits at breakfast, had begun shyly to talk about this. Others had drawn near, joined in; and we had expressed the wish that the talk could continue — and so decided on the spot to call a workshop. Posted a notice of it on the bulletin board. (Here is something I liked very much about Seneca — that we *could* freely improvise in this way.) A large number of women turned up at the time set — at the building you'll remember which is a small dome. But as we started round the circle, attention seemed scattered, and the talk meandering. It was Donna again who suggested we try another way of finding real listening. Her guess was that the subject was so fraught for each of us that we were feeling impatient for our turns — and so not quite able to hear those first in the circle. And they were unable to find their words because they felt unlistened to. She suggested that for a few minutes we turn, each, to the woman to the right or the left of us and, in twos for a while, spill out some of our feelings. And then go round the circle. So we did this. The tent was full of the rush of our voices — for what turned out to be many minutes. And then we went quietly round the circle and — there was at last real listening. And therefore speaking. As we told about our lives, there was a building awareness among us that the sexual energies which filled us often with painful anxieties were in fact a deep source of strength for us — if only we could rename them, honor them — slough from us the false naming, the despising of ourselves, which we had all been taught. Awareness, too, that we could give the name of "sexual" to this intense listening to one another which we were learning. Though we would be expanding the meaning of the word "sexual."

And if we would persist in learning how to be more fully our sexual selves in this uncommon sense — we could become empowered. I realize as I write these words that this will be the repeated theme of this letter to you.

But I am getting ahead of myself. For these two meetings of which I've just written took place toward the end of my stay at Seneca.

From the very first day I did begin to receive a happy sense of this new hope of empowerment. Would lie in bed at night musing about it. Without words. While the helicopter from the army depot churned noisily above us. Strong searchlight raking the camp. Afraid of us, afraid of us, I felt. Jane had joined me in the tent by now. (The Jane with whom I live. She'd driven up with friends, arriving a few hours after me.) We'd both sit up in our sleeping bags as the light entered our tent flap. Shake our heads at one another. It was like being stared at by some huge Peeping Tom. A reminder always that what I was finding cause for rejoicing was seen by the powers that be with very different eyes.

The second day after my arrival was to provide a more forceful reminder of this. By the end of that day (Saturday, the 30th) I found myself in a local jail — with 53 other women from the camp. Being frisked, being fingerprinted. In their hands now, and under their eyes, at closer range. No, not arrested by the Army; arrested by the sheriff of the town of Waterloo. But — the eye upon us somehow felt like much the same eye.

I'd had, in advance, no intention of getting arrested — on that day or any other day. For I wasn't sure that my 66-year-old body could any longer hold up very well in jail. And as you know, the walk we took that day was not planned as an act of civil disobedience. It was planned simply as a walk to the camp from Seneca Falls — which would have been a walk of about 15 miles; its intent, in the words of the statement we issued from jail, "to honor the great defiant women in our past who resisted

oppression, and to bring their courageous spirit to the Encampment." A number of those women were, of course,
women from this particular part of the country — Seneca
Falls, the home of Elizabeth Cady Stanton, and site of
the first Women's Rights Convention which she and
some other brave dissatisfied women from Seneca County brought about — in July of 1848. And Seneca County
had been a major stop on the underground railroad for
black slaves escaping to Canada. Harriet Tubman had
lived in a house near what was now the Army Depot. In
Seneca, too, women of the Iroquois Nation had met —
in 1590 — to demand an end to war among the different
tribes. We paused, in our walk, in front of the Wesleyan
Chapel where the Women's Rights Convention had been
held. The building is now the Seneca Falls laundromat.
Paused, in the next town, Waterloo, at the house where
the women's rights manifesto had been drafted, the "Declaration of Sentiments" — Mary Ann McClintock's house;
and then at the house of Jane Hunt, who had helped in
the drafting. At each stop a woman from the Women's
Rights National Historical Park (which is working to
preserve these buildings) told us quietly a little history.
We carried some beautiful cardboard portrait heads of
Stanton, of Tubman, of Lucretia Mott, of an Iroquois
woman.[2] We also, each of us, wore a bib on which we'd
written with magic markers the name of some woman —
from whatever place or time — whom we'd individually
chosen to honor for the life struggle she'd made. Quinn
wore the name of her great grandmother — "victim of
government persecution of pacifists." Quinn's friend
Rosalie wrote on her bib: "Jewish Lesbians Who Died
Resisting The Nazis." Jane wrote, "Emma Goldman." I'd
decided to write "Our Nameless." Blue wore no bib but
carried a banner with the name of Radclyffe Hall.

There were about 135 of us. Walking to honor our
women's history, written, unwritten. To honor in par-

ticular the history of women from this country. Not a very threatening walk, you might have thought. A walk staying carefully on the side of the road while on the highway; on the sidewalks through the towns. (Where we'd sometimes have to lower our banners or cardboard portrait heads so that they wouldn't catch in the overhanging branches of trees.) The sheriff had told us that we didn't even need a permit, as we weren't a parade. Yes, you might have thought that we'd be seen as harmless.

But the action of honoring our own history is *not* taken to be harmless. The stark truth is that we women are not supposed to look hard at that history. Not supposed to name our oppression or celebrate our struggle against it.

I began as we walked to pass out some of the purple-colored flyers for the walk, made by women from the New York branch of the Women's Pentagon Action. JULY 30 FEMINIST WALK — WE WILL CONNECT OUR WOMEN'S PAST TO OUR FEMINIST FUTURE. In your talk you quote a passage from this flyer which you think shows that we try to deny that men can be victims. You quote: "As women we know all too well the connection between militarism and the violence in our lives. The masculine ideal which the military perpetuates...is a concept of masculinity that victimizes *women, children and nature*." "My emphasis," you add. I agree that the writers could well have added "and of course a lot of men too." But — the very next passage in the flyer does read: "We know that the billions of dollars spent on weapons have left hundreds of thousands without jobs, decent housing or health care. We know that the powerful men who make these decisions make war *on us all*" (*my* emphasis), "especially women, people of color, the poor, the disabled and the elderly..." Didn't you notice these words? And didn't you notice that the very first paragraph in the flyer — which condemns the U.S. plan to deploy in Europe the new missiles stored at the Seneca Depot — says that we feel a responsibility to our European "sisters *and brothers* who have known generations of war on their soil?" (My emphasis.)

You don't really have to fear that women will forget — or forget ever for very long — that men, too, can be victims. What we women do have to fear is that we'll allow ourselves to deny, what for centuries and centuries — all the centuries of the patriarchy — we have been trained to deny: the fact that *we* have been victimized *as* women, victimized as a gender class (those whom men see themselves as not being). For though men have, of course, been oppressed too, it has not been *as men*. We are supposed to forget this. It is no accident that the chapel which housed our first women's rights gathering was allowed to become a laundromat. Just as it's no accident that the history of the murder of millions of uppity women as "witches" is un-taught in our schools. Witches, our children learn, are skinny old women with pointy hats who ride on broomsticks. At Halloween their half-scary half-funny silhouettes are hung around the classroom walls — and it's a night for fun. Norma, think of the denial that is sanctioned *here*. If we do *concentrate* now upon naming crimes against women, it has *taken* a very special concentration on our part to wake from the spell of the lie we are taught from birth: the grotesque lie that women are, as a gender class, *protected*. The lie that when we do find ourselves victimized it is an individual matter always, and if we look closely we'll discover that we've done something to bring it upon ourselves. Don't forget that only a very few years ago the existence of widespread battering of women was still a well-kept secret, as was the widespread sexual abuse of girls (yes, sometimes, though very much less frequently, of boys too) by fathers, stepfathers, uncles, older brothers. Only a few years ago, rape was still spoken of as though it could be fun. And we women weren't good sports if we couldn't speak of it that way ourselves. I can remember singing along with friends, to a lighthearted tune, words by Noel Coward I think: "Violate me in violet time in the vilest way that you know-o-o-o!...Please on me no mercy show-o-o-o!" Can you think of any crimes against men that have been denied in this way — that have been treated as if they didn't even happen?

So — we went walking down the road, taking our oppression as fact, taking it seriously now, taking our struggle against it seriously, and taking seriously the connection between the war against women and the threat of nuclear war which could destroy us all. We shouldn't really have been surprised that we walked into big trouble.

The sheriff had told us that we didn't need a permit. He'd told us also — told the women making arrangements for the walk — that a few Vietnam vets in the town of Waterloo were full of anger toward us and had talked about blockading us. He said he'd persuaded them to abandon this crazy plan and to agree simply to stand at the side of the road as our walk went by and let us know how they felt about us.

As we left Seneca Falls — after forming a circle in a park near the church in which we'd gathered, after singing for a while, and glancing round the circle to read the names of the women whose spirits we were honoring — our processing was calm and cheerful, and the police were giving us a courteous escort. We began to hand out leaflets. Some of the people to whom I offered mine accepted them gladly, some refused them, but with no particular energy, with looks of quiet disdain. But I did keep thinking about the vets we would encounter in a few miles, and trying to prepare myself to face their anger. I tried to imagine in advance how they would be. Saw them lined up by the side of the road. Would one or more be disabled vets, in wheelchairs? They'd be holding American flags, I was sure. And their faces would be bitter, bitter. Wounded or not in body, casualties of that abominable war. I began to pick wildflowers that grew along the sidewalks — the chicory and Queen Anne's Lace I had drummed a greeting to the days I'd first been walking to the camp. And when we paused at Jane Hunt's house, I made an effort to pass the suggestion down the line that we offer flowers to the bitter men. I had begun to worry that the mood of the walk was too relaxed. To wish that in our circle we had talked for a while about what we might be walking into.

As we drew close to the business center of Waterloo, we began to see more flags stuck out on lawns, and more people now refused our leaflets. A few drivers yelled at us from their cars. One woman driver whom I approached as she waited at a light waved me back angrily and yelled, "You're assholes!" I managed a half-smile and a shrug. Then told myself — to cheer myself — that I could have replied that assholes are much maligned; what would we do without them? But no, she wouldn't have appreciated the observation.

And then across the street I saw Penny in her car driving slowly back from the front of the walk. Penny is the friend with whom Jane had driven up from Florida. She'd volunteered this morning to drive her car as a support car. When she caught sight of me, she leaned out the window and called out, rolling her eyes, "It's wild up there."

I can still hear those words in my ears. See her rolling her large eyes. Receive in my solar plexus the abrupt knowledge that the encounter which I'd been fantasizing was a shadow of the reality that actually waited for us just ahead.

I had dropped back toward the end of the walk, because sometimes my leafletting took me across lawns and up steps. I hurried forward now. Passed Blue and paused to mutter, "We'll be needing to keep our calm" and quoted Penny's words to her. The sixties had taught me a little about how *to* keep calm in the face of an angry group. And I worried as I hurried along: Few of the women on this walk would have had any such experience. I needn't have worried about that, I realize now. Every woman learns something of the skill of keeping calm in the face of male anger — has to learn this just to survive daily life.

I'd been taking pleasure in my leafletting — recovering the art I'd learned years ago from walks through the south, art of finding within myself just the attitude of friendliness and expectancy that could sometimes move a person who was about to refuse a leaflet to take it after all. But I stopped handing out any leaflets now. Though the sidewalk along which I hurried was full of towns-people standing in the doorways of shops, standing right there; and I could have offered a few without slowing my pace. Glancing into their faces, I saw a look that told me: Better not — a rigor in each face, a rigor in each stiff body, that told me my gesture would be taken as a provocation. So I pulled the batch of leaflets back toward my chest.

As I did so I felt within me a flick of sharp fear. And then a deeper fear still: the fear of my fear. For I'd only be safe, I knew — we would all only be safe — if we could manage not to let our fear be visible.

That look which had made me pull back — look of fixity — was the look of people who are not quite there *within* their bodies, not quite *able* to accept something on their own. They seemed to have given up mind and impulse to some large Mind — or Non-Mind, larger Presence that waited up ahead. I couldn't see that massed presence yet, but I see that they knew it was there; it had their spell-bound attention. And now I began to hear the sound of it. Sound of many voices. Not the tumult familiar to me from the camp — rising and falling tumult of distinctive notes. This was the monotonous very unpleasant voice of a mob.

And now I could hear the words yelled: a thudded accent on each yelled word. GO HOME, COMMIES! GO HOME,

commies! nuke'm till they glow! nuke'm till they glow!
I walked past the same words chalked on the side of a
garage. But didn't see them. They were reported to me
later by other women on the walk. NUKE'M TILL THEY
GLOW, THEN SHOOT'M IN THE DARK! My eyes were somewhere else, were straight ahead of me, I guess. And then
I saw the people who were yelling. Massed on the bridge,
where the road begins to lead out of town — a bridge over
a small river whose waters I never did look at, either. I
don't know whether it was wide or narrow, ran swift or
slow. They were massed deeply, across the full width of
the bridge.[3] Two hundred, three hundred people, perhaps — most of them men (in shirt sleeves, in under-
shirts), but women too, and even a few children. Shaking
American flags. Jabbing the air with the pointy flag
poles. We all agreed later that the flags seemed like
brandished weapons. At some point during the two or
three hours in which we faced this crowd, something
made me glance down, and I thought I saw a spent car-
tridge on the ground. When I picked it up, I saw it was
one of those pointed ends of a flag staff. But there were
real cartridges on some of those men. Judith has snap-
shots showing the bulge of a concealed holster on two or
three of them. One man with a gun was disarmed by the
police as he lunged toward some of us. I didn't see this
myself. Saw the end of the incident on video. The man
on the ground, the police wrestling with him. I can't
make out whether or not he is a man I saw almost at
once — at some distance from me — as I arrived at the
bridge. A man with a flushed contorted face, the woman
with him clutching, clawing at his chest — her hands, eyes
pleading. Was it soon after this that he drew his gun and
lunged? Or was he not the armed man? I felt I had to give
my attention to angry ones closer to me, for there I had
the best chance of having some calming effect. If I — if
we — could make eye contact with first one individual
and then another, and start conversations with some of

them, it might help them to remember, that they *were* individuals, and not mere members of a mob. All about me I could see that other women too were attempting this. Were looking into the eyes of one, then another. Sometimes speaking, sometimes simply facing the other steadily. How beautiful I thought these women's faces. I *see* them still. No fear written on them. No hostility. And a lovely stubbornness written on each face. I remember certain women, of course, especially. Jane. As she first glanced all about her, to take her bearings. Blue. Blue was talking, talking. So was Vera, whom you know from the War Resisters League. And I remember Judith, standing tall and still and calm. Though at one point when I looked toward her she was standing with her back to the mob, staring into space. She told me later that she couldn't look at the crowd any longer without betraying agitation. I don't think she ever did let it be visible.

One of the first times I turned to look behind me, to see what was happening there, I saw that a number of women had sat down, then formed a circle together. Quinn was one of the first to take this action. I can remember the reassurance I felt at once, at the sight of those quietly seated figures. Without words they made the statement it was essential that we make. The statement that we posed no threat—had no intention of trying to thrust our way through the mob. But the statement that we had no intention of retreating, either. We knew our Constitutional rights. We had a right to walk here. The two-fold message that gives nonviolent struggle its leverage: We won't be bullied; but you needn't fear us. You needn't fear us; but we won't be bullied. And they made another statement, too: We were going to share our thoughts and feelings in the midst of this crisis. Base any decisions to be made upon that sharing. Knowing that some of us were seated in that quiet, deliberative circle made it easier for me to stand facing the townspeople. And I think the fact that some of us stood eye to

[213

eye with the mob made it easier for them to sit there. Each group loaned the other added strength — helped the other to feel a bit less vulnerable.

I began to attempt some conversations with the flag wavers. I had at first chosen simply to stand, looking into faces, and holding high my own flag — the bouquet of chicory and Queen Anne's Lace I had picked. If felt that *this* spoke for us without words. Said — again — that they needn't fear us. Said, too, that we gave our deepest allegiance not just to the particular nation in which we'd been born, but to a wider world, the world of nature itself which all of us everywhere could name our homeland — threatened now with extinction. "Those are just weeds!" one of the men yelled at me. Blue, overhearing, began a patient but vehement explanation to him of all the wonderful practical uses of chicory. "They're wilted!" another man yelled. They had indeed wilted under the mid-day sun. But I persist in believing, however, that their meaning was not entirely lost on the men who yelled their words of scorn.

Flags and allegiance were of course a frequent subject of the conversations in which we engaged that afternoon. I'm sure you've heard of the incident involving The Flag that took place a few days before the camp's formal July 4th opening — when a man from Waterloo arrived at the camp, flag in hand, and told the organizers in effect: Fly this on your front lawn or else — I'll tell the world about it. A meeting was called — of all the women then at the camp — to decide what response to make to this. And the meeting went on for many hours, for there were many different feelings to be listened to. Consensus was finally reached that the camp shouldn't fly this particular flag — which hadn't exactly been offered as a gift, but any woman could fly any flag that she chose to make herself. Many flags were made that day and the next, some of them very beautiful works of embroidery. Flags that were for Peace and Justice, flags of the Tree of Life, flags that spoke for all our visions. Several women chose to make and fly flags that were the Stars and Stripes. In spite of which the rumor was spread that we refused to fly our country's flag and had spit and peed upon the one offered us.

So there on the bridge at Waterloo the question was asked us again and again: Why don't we love our country? The question within that question, I'd say: Why don't we love the patriarchy? And much of our talk an attempt to draw a distinction between these two — arguing that we could best act out of love of our country by challenging it to make some necessary changes. I asked one of the grimacing men who blocked our way: If he had a child whom he loved... "I *have* a child!" he cut in. Well, if that child were behaving in a way that he thought very wrong, did he feel that he would show his love for him better by saying in effect, "Anything you do is OK with me" or by trying to change the way in which he was behaving. The man squinted at me, silent for a few moments. I had the feeling he was considering my words. I remember even that I was able to reach out and touch his arm lightly without his flinching. But then he gave a little jerk to his head. As if recalled to duty. And — eyes glazed again — he thrust his flag at me. Would I hold the flag? Certainly, I told him — taking it; it was my flag as well as his. Would he hold mine? And I held out to him my bunch of wild flowers. He snatched them from me, then quickly let them drop to the ground, laughing a strange false laugh, "Oh they dropped!" Then, as I stooped to recover them, snatched back his flag.

1 Speech given at the October 3, 1983 forum in New York City on Feminist Organizing in the Peace Movement, printed in *The Guardian* October 19, 1983.

2 The Native American woman was not of the Iroquois tribe. She was Sarah Winnemucca of the Piute tribe. Her Indian name was Thoc-me-tony, or "Shellflower" in English.

3 Barbara's note: Being in a state of shock led to this faulty memory of the position of the crowd on the bridge. I would have corrected it if I'd had the strength.

INTERVIEW WITH BARBARA DEMING

THE SENECA WOMEN'S PEACE
ENCAMPMENT, AUGUST 4, 1983,
BY THE BOSTON WOMEN'S
VIDEO COLLECTIVE

INTERVIEWER: Barbara, you just spent five days in the Interlaken Junior High School, which was a makeshift jail. Could you tell me how you got there and what your experience there meant to you?

BARBARA: Right. Well, I got there by sitting down at the bridge in Waterloo when a group of, I think it was about 200, townspeople — though they'd promised the sheriff that they were not going to blockade our walk — did do that. A walk in celebration of some of the great women of the last wave of feminism, some of them from around this part of the country, who had in fact made their part of the country famous. So you might say that it was ironic in a way that the townspeople wanted to stop this walk which was celebrating part of their history, really. But I would say that their perception of us was really very accurate. A few women, I'm afraid, felt dismay when we sat down at that bridge, when the sheriff wanted us just to go away; he wanted us to do just what the townspeople did. They were shouting at us, "go away, go away" and that's what he tried to tell us, too, though he'd originally given us permission to walk.

INTERVIEWER: Why did the women decide not to go away, even though the townspeople were yelling, "Go home" and "Go away"?

BARBARA: I could give several answers to that. In the first place, of course, our most basic constitutional rights were being flouted. We had an absolute right, which the sheriff had admitted, to walk through that town. Simple freedom of speech — one reason that I sat down and didn't go away. There were also, I think, safety reasons. The crowd really was threatening — and we all felt it was — so we sat down. We sat down for two reasons. We sat down to diffuse their violence because, though we were saying we have a right to do this, we were also saying we're not going to thrust our way through you. Actually if we had turned and retreated, we would have been in much more danger.

But to go back to how the crowd perceived us, I think they perceived us very accurately as a threat to patriarchal power. One thing that makes me feel that our action there on the bridge is very deeply connected with our actions at the Depot — and very deeply connected to our reason for being here as women only, an encampment of women — is because actually if we were just there at the Depot saying, "Nuclear weapons are a threat to us all," there's no reason why we couldn't/shouldn't be men and women. Many men feel that too. I think what distinguishes us here is that we have almost all of us the feminist vision that we're never going to end war unless we dissolve the patriarchy. And I think the crowd at the bridge recognized, not consciously but unconsciously, that that's precisely what we're saying.

I heard Blue Lunden say to one person interviewing her, that the things that they were screaming at us were very significant. She made, I thought, a beautiful analysis of it. They were saying, "Go home, commies;" "Go home, Jews;" "Nuke the lezzies." Sometimes they also said "Kill the Jews," or "Let's see some blood." And Blue said that when they said, "Go home, commies"—most of them don't even know what communism is—but they saw another form of government. When they said, "Go home, Jews," they saw another form of religion. When they said, "Nuke the lezzies," they saw another form of sexuality. So in a certain sense, they were very perceptive even though they were out of their minds.

INTERVIEWER: Do you think the villagers, then, had good reason to feel threatened? Do you think they will lose if women do become more powerful, and if lesbians and Jews become more powerful? Do you think people who are men and Christians and heterosexuals will lose something?

BARBARA: No. What I was trying to say in my statement at court was that they were fearing us. That's why both the villagers were full of fear of us—and why they were threatening us—and those who arrested us were full of fear of us and that's why they arrested us. But I said in court that they have really no need to fear us. It's true that we want to change everything utterly, so they will lose what they now think they need, which is control, power, ownership of women's bodies, ownership of the land. The lie of ownership has them intoxicated. But one thing that was thrilling to me about both what happened on the bridge and what happened in the jail was that the process we set in motion to protect ourselves and to guide us in how we should behave was a process which is the opposite of what they now have. It is the opposite of hierarchy, the opposite of ownership. And what thrilled me was that as they observed it, I could see them begin to respect it and begin to not feel threatened by it and this is our message to them. Our message is, we're going to utterly change the process of our lives and don't be scared of it. It's going to take from you what you think

[219

you need, but you don't need it. So even at the bridge there, I think the fact that they saw us sit down — what we did, I thought, worked so well. Some of us sat down in a circle, and some of us continued to face them and to talk with them. And in the circle they could see us — even in this dangerous situation in which the police kept trying to rush us and make us feel we had to decide instantly, we insisted on not making any decision until each woman had a voice. And I was surprised right then at how much the police consented to wait. They, in spite of themselves, respected this process. They could have said, "Tell me right now!" and we would have had to do it right now in a certain sense. They started out saying that, but as soon as we ignored the ultimatum and just insisted on this process, they respected it.

It was the same in another instance that to me was so dramatic. When the authorities at the jail discovered that two women had escaped out the window, they panicked. They panicked because their authority had been flouted and they had to reassert their authority and their power. With the women guards who'd been guarding us, we'd begun to establish real friendships and they had begun to respect us, again, watching our process. Even they, when the man entered the scene — and he wasn't a sheriff, I forget his exact demonination — and they, of course, could feel their jobs at risk and you could understand why they were panicky, but their faces changed. Suddenly this rigidity entered and we were ordered out to the halls, even though we were half dressed and it was very cold out there and they were being very strict and very ungentle with us. We were out there in the halls while they searched the rooms. This was so, so wild because first they did a count, then they did a count again, then they did a count *again*. Yet obviously two were missing. Then they began to look under the beds and they looked under the beds again. Then they began to look in corners where women couldn't possibly be hiding. For a while it was comic, except we all knew it was going to turn from comedy to something very unfunny very soon. So we waited for that and as soon as we were out in the hall, we knew that another scene had begun. The voices became very harsh. And for a while we lost it and began to yell a little back and forth. Yelled that it was cold and could we have blankets? No, we coudn't. And why not?

And then something happened that was very scary and it was especially scary for the Jewish women among us because it just reverberated so of the concentration camps. I think it also reverberated in any woman there of the witch persecutions because it became so irrational. At a certain point they'd already searched the rooms; now we were to be taken back into the rooms one by one and our bodies were to be searched and the women put on rubber gloves. As soon as I saw the women put on rubber gloves, a sense of terror invaded me because I thought what they were doing, whether they recognized it or not, they were going to look for those women in our bodies. So it took me right back to the witch persecution mentality and of course it took the Jewish women in our midst right back into the concentration camps.

But what happened here, too, is we began to calm down and follow *our* process of asking them reasonable questions, like "Do you think you can find these missing women in our vaginas?" We began to say, "Why are you punishing us for what two people who are not present have done?" And we began to ask all kinds of pertinent questions and not yell at them, but take our familiar turn in asking them and waiting for their reply, turning the thing into one of these meetings where each person is allowed to speak. They began to calm down and by the end of it, *because* we'd re-established that process, and even though they'd been on the point of — well, they'd dragged one woman already and the mood was rush, rush, force this on us — but they began to both respect and, I think, be grateful for our process which enabled

[221

them to come out of this mood of just cuckoo-ness. At the end of it, the man who was some kind of sub-sheriff, he ended by — he had to asset, "Well, this is the last kind act I'm going to perform."

We were allowed to walk back into the room without any search. When he had said, "This is the last kind act," he started out by saying, "We've been very kind to you, you know. We have given you good food." And that's one of the points when the women began to say, "You say you've been kind, but we shouldn't be here at all." You know, to make these points. But, as I say, what was so thrilling to me was to discover — and what gave me such hope for the future — is to see that they too were grateful when we established another process. And I would say this process *is* what the end of patriarchy is and I would like to find more and more ways of saying to them, "Look, don't be scared of us, because what has just happened and what you were grateful that happened is all that we're trying to bring into being."

INTERVIEWER: The scenario you just described in prison sounds really incredible and that the process not only transformed yourselves in some way but also your imprisoners. But I have a question about hierarchy and consensus, or lack of hierarchy and consensus, that is the norm here, but is not the norm out in society. It seems like in a society the size of the Encampment, perhaps it can work through/with consensus and without hierarchy. Can that work in a larger community, in a city, in New York City, in the United States? Do you think it can work and how?

BARBARA: I have no doubt that it can work; but when you say how, I think it has continually to be invented. We had to continually invent it inside that room. There were times when we'd lose it and then we'd discuss how we'd lost it and how there was something we had to invent.

For instance, when we learned that the two women had escaped, most of the discussions we had were completely open discussions and we were glad that the women guards were listening because we felt they too were learning from it and they too were learning what we were like. And it was interesting that in the beginning they would interrupt our meetings with yells of who was to go for a shower or something. But after we asked them, you know, not to interrupt it with the yells, they began to come and they'd stand there for a moment and wait for a moment even if they had some news they had to give us — wait for a moment that wasn't such an interruption and say, "Excuse me, but..." There were times when it couldn't be open because it might put someone in jeopardy if we were open; so we had to invent, try to invent, a way in which you'd form smaller circles and then someone from the smaller circle would ask someone else to form another circle and discuss it.

A lot of people would have said that we couldn't afford that process in *our* situation. We had, was it 53 women? Often decisions had to be made you would think very quickly, and you would say it would have been quicker if we'd delegated a few women who we'd trust to make these decisions. It would have been infinitely quicker and it wouldn't have worked. It wouldn't have represented us. And I think the same is true in the larger society. It will always look — some people will always say you can't afford to give everyone a voice; there isn't time. But I would say all the time spent in doing it faster is wasted time because the decisions you come out with aren't the right decisions.

But, it has to be invented, you know. Just as, for instance, some times we'd just go around the circle taking turns. Sometimes we'd have what was called a floating chair — one woman would speak then people would raise hands and the woman who'd just spoken would call on one of the raised hands. Or sometimes if there was time pressure — a lawyer, for instance, would only be there for 10 minutes and had to have an answer — we'd choose a facilitator who had some experience and who'd try to keep the thing to the issue in a specially concentrated way. And there you would use people who'd had a little more experience.

Oh, there was one fascinating moment when the court hearing was coming up and if we won the right to be seen as a group (the judge couldn't hear each one of us), we were going to have to have representatives. And the question was, how to choose them? And it started out with a few women nominating certain people who they thought were especially articulate. A few women had been suggested and someone objected and said, "This isn't the way we've been doing things. At this point, we trust any woman in this group to speak for us and this is getting hierarchical again." We went around the circle to see how people felt about this. Most people were willing to trust any woman, especially since some of the women already had said that they wouldn't trust themselves.[1] So we decided on drawing lots just out of a hat. And if any woman would feel that she didn't want to do this, she could withdraw her name. This to me was really putting it to the test, you know. The strange thing that happened was that when we did draw numbers from the hat, some of the numbers were of women who said they were sorry they might just faint or they would rather not; so another number would be called. The mysterious thing was that at least two of the numbers that finally came up were two of the women who had first been called upon to represent us. But again and again, we'd be tempted to do it the old way but then finally insist on doing it this every-woman-has-a-voice way. The more we thought about it, the more everybody would become happy with that way.

INTERVIEWER: Can you think of any examples of how decisions have been made at the Encampment where this

224]

consensus process has been subverted and not — and the solutions have not been successfully reached?

BARBARA: I'm not the one to speak to that because I think it was the day after I arrived here that I sat down at the bridge. And though I've heard some stories about how there hasn't been this process, I don't think it makes sense just to speak at second-hand.

INTERVIEWER: But you do feel — it sounds like you feel very positive about the process that happened in prison and also prior to going to jail. And do you feel that the kind of process will continue here? And are you going to be part of it?

BARBARA: I'm not sure how much longer I'll stay. Partly because I'm not sure how much longer my body can go without going back home and deeply resting. I'm tempted just to stay on and on and on. Also, I want to go home and try and write and I'll have to gauge how much I'll forget of the experience in jail if I don't go home and start taking notes soon.

---

1 Barbara's note: When I heard these words of mine later, they jolted me.

APPENDIX

We are a diverse group of 54 women from throughout America who on July 30, 1983, began a peace walk along with 75 of our sisters. We set out from Seneca Falls, New York, to the Women's Peace Encampment in Romulus. Our purpose was to honor the great, defiant women in our past who have resisted oppression and to bring their courageous spirit to the Encampment.

In the small town of Waterloo, four miles into our walk, our way was blocked by several hundred townspeople brandishing American flags and chanting, "Commies, go home!" To diffuse the potential violence, many of us sat down in the classic tradition of nonviolence to discuss what to do. Others of us faced the mob, speaking calmly to individuals. One man said to one of us, "If more people here understood what you're saying to me, this wouldn't be happening. There is a lot of misinformation." Gradually, the tension began to subside.

Although this trouble had been anticipated, when we were actually confronted, police protection proved grossly inadequate. The police did take care to protect us from the more violent members of the community, but certain of the Sheriff's orders in fact served to excite tensions. For example, while we were sitting, the Sheriff

[227

announced that if we did not disperse, we would be charged with inciting a riot. At these words, the crowd became truly menacing. The chanting swelled into a roar, and the crowd surged forward, thrusting their pointed two-foot flag poles at us. People on the sidelines kept insisting that our actions would lead to conquest by the Russians and the denial of our freedoms as Americans. Ironically, they now were threatening our freedom with the flag that was to them the very symbol of freedom. It was also ironic that they were incensed by our response to their blockade, since the blockade itself was a classic — albeit far from nonviolent — protest tactic.

Aware of the danger of our situation, most of us sat down to help diffuse the violence and to discuss what to do. It was hard to do this, as we also had to cope with fear for our lives. This was not hysteria on our part. The general police appraisal of the crowd was that women could try to pass through the crowd but they would surely "be massacred." Flowers were thrown into our midst and when we sniffed them we found they had been sprayed with mace. We prepared then for the possibility of teargas by holding moistened cloths over our noses. The announcement of our imminent arrest came more frequently over the bullhorn, and the Sheriff pressured us to take an alternative route. We discussed this possibility, but realized that turning our backs to the crowd would put us in greater danger. Moreover, we wanted to stand firm in our constitutional right to pass through the town and complete our walk.

At one point, the police succeeded in making the crowd retreat about 20 feet and some of them suggested we might be able to get through on the sidewalk. The instant we stood and tried to do so, the crowd moved back in and the police began arresting us, even hand-cuffing a few of us. During the arrest, as some police tried to carry women without hurting them, they were egged on to hurt the women by the crowd's shouts of "Drag her, drag her." In all, four truck loads of us were deposited at the Seneca County Jail by 3:30 that afternoon, including Millie, a respected local resident who had joined us when she saw the obvious injustice of our arrest. Other townspeople expressed support for us by sending fruit and beverages to us that evening.

In resistance to this injustice, we refused to give our names during the processing, and refused to post bail. Though we had been taken in on a violation, "disorderly conduct," we were fingerprinted and photographed. Our court hearing was not set until August 3, four days later.

Our intent was to walk, not to do civil disobedience. We sat to diffuse the violence, to decide our course, and to make the denial of our constitutional rights clear. One of the things we love most about our country is the Bill of Rights. These rights were denied when the police tried to disperse us and when they arrested us instead of the people threatening us. If we had retreated, we would have neglected to honor our country's most democratic mandate. That Saturday, everything was pushed to its most rapid, confusing and expensive conclusion.

The taunts from the crowd were "Nuke the Lezzies," "Go Home Commies," "Kill the Jews," "Throw them off the bridge, let's see some blood." Among us are many lesbians. There are Jewish women. Almost all of us would call ourselves feminists. Most of us have various beliefs in economic or social change that people label communist, socialist, anarchist.

All of us, whatever we are, deeply feel that our civil rights to be any of these — lesbian, Jewish, feminist, critical of our country — were violated. And further, our civil rights as citizens, to walk free of terror through any town in our own land and express our views and feelings, were trampled.

We know that many of our perhaps unwitting persecutors feel strongly about the flag of our country as expressed in "My country, may she always be right, but right or wrong — my country." Yet trapped by their fear, their hatred, their unfamiliarity of lesbians, Jewish people, radicals, feminists, they missed our efforts as Americans, just as they are, to right our country's wrongs.

And it is exactly two of those major wrongs that we had come to protest — the nuclear weapons in their backyard and our position as women. As women we know all too well the connection between militarism and the violence in our lives. The masculine ideal which the military perpetuates encourages force, dominance, power and violence. It is a concept of masculinity that victimizes women, children and nature.

At this writing we are still being held at Interlaken Junior High School. Group solidarity grows stronger by the hour, and we remain undaunted in our determination to stop the nuclear weapons and save life on our planet.

Photo: Jane Gapen

Barbara leafletting on the walk from Seneca Falls, that was stopped in Waterloo. This photo was a favorite of Barbara's because it showed her long stride.

Barbara Deming, poet, story writer, essayist and journalist, was born in 1917 in New York City. She spent the last years of her life in the Florida Keys with the writer and painter Jane Gapen, and a community of other women. She died in 1984.

She was active in the nonviolent civil rights and antiwar struggles of the 1960's and visited North Vietnam during the war. She put her hopes for change above all in the nonviolent struggles of the feminist movement.

She was a lesbian from the age of sixteen. She recognised the struggle to hold to her pride in this sexual self, as her earliest political struggle. She wrote six other books including *We Are All Part of One Another, a Barbara Deming Reader* (1983, New Society Press) and *A Humming Under My Feet* (1985, The Women's Press, London).

SPINSTERS INK

Change The Future With Books That Change Women's Lives

Spinsters Ink, a women's independent publishing house, has been producing quality, innovative books of women's art, literature, and non-fiction since 1978. Our commitment is to publishing works that are beyond the scope of mainstream commercial publishers: books that not only name crucial issues in women's lives, but also demonstrate healing and change.

Spinsters publishes books that flourish between the cracks of what will be accepted — and what can be imagined.

Your support, through buying our books or investing in other ways in the company, enables us to bring out new books, books that keep helping women envision and create the kinds of worlds in which we all can live.

For a complete list of our titles, or a brochure explaining our investment plans, please write to us.

Spinsters Ink
P.O. Box 410687
San Francisco, CA 94141